SHARPENED IRON

The Tee Cotton Bowl Story

Sharpened Iron © 2010 Mel LeCompte Jr.
All photographs are © of their respective owners, credited and published with permission.

DEDICATION

Sharpened Iron is dedicated to Alan de la Villisbret and James 'Baggy' Latiolais.

Alan, I can still hear the laugh that rocked the old Daily World building.

Coach Latch, I really hope you're good at making predictions.

CONTENTS

FOREWORD..i

PREFACE..v

CHAPTER ONE:
    Hakas, Hail Marys, and Hallelujahs.....................................1

CHAPTER TWO
    A Busy Day for the Good Doctor.......................................26

CHAPTER THREE
    E.T. Winds Up in a Sauce...57

CHAPTER FOUR
    The Game That Should Not Exist.....................................75

CHAPTER FIVE
    Building the Old School..98

CHAPTER SIX
    We Had Food Attached..113

CHAPTER SEVEN
    Tim Brings the Umbrella...131

CHAPTER EIGHT
    Sacred Heart Becomes Sacred Ground.........................145

CHAPTER NINE
    Showtime..161

CHAPTER TEN
    A Peek Into the Future...175

EPILOGUE...185

APPENDIX
    Photos, records, credits, and web links............................191

FOREWORD

How did a Panther from Delcambre, Louisiana end up in a relationship with the great home of the Sacred Heart Trojans and Ville Platte Bulldogs and the incredible *Tee Cotton Bowl*?

It was a meeting of fate between 'Doctor' Tim Fontentot and myself 1300 miles away in Atlantic City at the 73rd annual Maxwell Football Club Awards banquet. Now, the words "from Delcambre" and "banquet in Atlantic City" are an obvious oxymoron. The phrases go together about as much as "black tie affair" and *"fais do-do"*.

Our small motley crew of Bayou State Maxwell Clubbers managed to turn Atlantic City more into Morgan City, with each of us decked out in Mardi Gras beads and light-up fleur de lis, toting our New Orleans Saints banners.

We definitely kept the Super Bowl party going in New Jersey that March.

There we were, ten diehard New Orleans Saints fans in the middle of Atlantic City watching our very own hero Drew Brees accept the Maxwell Football Club's Professional Player of the Year award (aka the *Bert Bell* award) in person. We all had our Saints beads, glowing goblets and Saints Super Bowl banners.

It was Mardi Gras in a twelve-foot radius.

To say we were being noticed is an understatement. Anytime Drew Brees, Coach Payton or the Saints were mentioned at the banquet, the reaction from our table was like us reliving Garrett Hartley kicking our way into the Super Bowl! We poured our enthusiasm into this banquet, and the natives loved us for it. The highlight of the night was Drew Brees pointing to our table and explaining to the attendees that his success is because of Saints fans like us.

The only analogy that comes to mind is the popular television commercial: The airplane ticket to Atlantic City, hotel room, food, and tickets to the MFC annual awards dinner costs money. But Drew Brees pointing in our direction and making that statement to rabid Cajun Who Dat fans? *Priceless!*

Anyway, I fell in love with the TCB not long after we arrived back home from the ceremony, while holding extensive meetings with the Fontenots. I soon realized that Tim Fontenot, the Tee Cotton founder, could sell Holy Water to the Devil himself. He did not have to preach very long before I was buying into the concept of this special game.

Many prep teams have rivalry games played within their city limits. This would undoubtedly be just another one of those games right? I figured the TCB was loved by the local community for obvious reasons, but probably nothing more than an average intra-city championship.

Boy, was I wrong.

Average high school games are not featured by *NFL Films*. I am pretty sure that most prep rivalries have not been blessed by Pope John Paul II.

The TCB brings high schools with social, ethnic, and religious differences and creates an amazing event the whole town, state, and country can be proud of.

This past year, I was indeed fortunate to have two amazing football organizations cross my path – the Maxwell Football Club on a national level and the Tee Cotton Bowl on a local level. Together, these two great organizations honor excellence as well as good sportsmanship.

The Maxwell Club is the oldest and most prestigious football club in the country. I made it my mission to get the first ever satellite chapter awarded right here in Louisiana, where football is like Fat Tuesday each weekend in the fall. With more NFL players per capita (according to *USA Football*), we are indeed a football state.

The Louisiana Chapter of the MFC looks forward to growing right alongside with the Tee Cotton Bowl in promoting and honoring football in our communities and state, while bringing attention to the great history of the Louisiana football tradition on a national level.

Brian Campbell
Louisiana chapter founder and president
Maxwell Football Club

PREFACE

I still remember when I got the assignment.

It was fall of 2001. While teaching a crew of middle-schoolers was my 'real job', I managed to worm my way onto the sports desk at the Opelousas *Daily World* newspaper during Louisiana moonlight.

One afternoon while rolling out of my classroom and into the *World*, sports editor (and Zydeco historian extraordinaire) Herman Fuselier grabbed me.

"Hey Mel," he chimed, "There's this guy in Ville Platte who keeps calling – Dr. Tim Fontenot. He puts on this thing called the Tee Cotton Bowl. You wanna go?"

At least that's what Herman probably said. All I heard was, "You wanna make that payment on that Camaro of yours?"

I paused for a moment. See, I was a New Orleans native who'd been transplanted to the middle of Acadiana via the spell of a Cajun woman. I was a certified city boy, and Opelousas easily fit my definition of a country town.

Just one McDonald's? Just one Wal-Mart? Just one interstate? Opelousas certainly sounded rural enough to me.

I was still getting used to my newly adopted home. How dare my boss ask me to leave my comfort zone and travel 20 miles deeper into Cajun country.

Could Acadiana get much more rural?

I wasn't sure that I wanted to find out.

But, like a trooper, I went to Tee Cotton II as assigned. I diligently meandered state highways of questionable construction while avoiding legendary Louisiana potholes and stereotypically posthumous opossum to reach my destination.

Once I arrived, I suspected that I'd landed in an alternate universe.

I'd made it to a place where schools let out for 'Cajun Passover'. The town radio station broadcasted in French. The most notable landmark was a half-century old independent record shop that to this day still holds its own in a world of iPods and *Pandora*.

Dorothy had Oz. I had Ville Platte.

I settled into Ville Platte High's stadium to witness this city championship between the local public school and its cross-town Catholic rival, Sacred Heart. Claiming my chair in the press box, I accidentally kicked an object in front of me. I glanced down.

"Oh, great," I thought to myself as I looked at an empty bottle that once held hard liquor of frugal design, "What have I gotten myself into."

But that little first impression was quickly flushed out by the hospitality of those around me, who made fun of said container and how it may have found itself there. Clearly, the other inhabitants of the box were as surprised as I – if not twice as upset – that such an item would wind up on their campus.

As we joked the incident away, a determined, small-framed man entered the room. He quickly fiddled with a few objects in the back of the press box, and just as swiftly exited. The stealthy gentleman was as quiet as a mouse and nimble as a shoemaker's elf as he went about.

"That was Tim Fontenot," someone muttered to me.

Before that someone could finish their sentence and I could properly introduce myself, he was gone. The same man that quietly invaded the room was now down on the field, his smile hidden under an FDNY baseball cap.

Dr. Tim took command of a makeshift stage on the right side of the field where he honored the local police and fire departments. With the shadow of 9/11 still casting even on the most rural areas, the good doctor was beginning the process of healing the wounds in his hometown.

After the pre-game presentation, I turned around to get a better view of the object Dr. Tim originally came inside to fuss with. It was a giant bowl best described to people up north as a slightly squatty Stanley Cup doppelganger, and to those in the Deep South as that fancy gumbo pot you'd serve out of when the 'good company' came around.

Impressive.

In fact, the Tee Cotton trophy was almost as impressive as all the other small strokes Dr. Fontenot used when imagining the event. He made sure this was more than a football game. This was a celebration of competition and community for a tiny Cajun countryside preserved from the modern plagues that corrode larger cities. This was a display of patriotic songs, fire trucks and American flags for a small town still reeling in the aftershock and uncertainty of 9/11.

In the shadow of our nation's dark hour, Dr. Tim certainly had the correct touch. Every extra flourish just seemed sincere. Neither overdone nor understated, every part of Tee Cotton II – patriotic gestures included – just felt right.

I left the game in a bit of awe.

My Camaro was pulling me out of the stadium parking lot and back to the reality of my sports desk when I found out that Ville Platte wasn't done with me yet. The town left me with a final souvenir – a flat tire. Not a half-mile past the stadium, I was standing on the sidewalk of Main Street, with a shredded slab of rubber tread just mocking me and my deadline.

Someday, history may possibly declare that flat tire as the most important flat tire in the history of Louisiana prep sports.

As my car and I stood stranded on the side of the street, two police officers just happened to pass by. More courteous than their young ages and paychecks probably required them to be, they hurriedly worked out a plan. It was decided that one would keep me company as the other ran to his friend's house to borrow a lug wrench.

The officer not only went to his buddy's house but also woke him up to help forage for the tool. Once he returned, both cops were on their knees at the Camaro's altar, helping me wrestle off a stubborn rear passenger-side rim.

What was this? Friendly police officers going above and beyond their job description? Hanging around to keep a total stranger company? Waking a friend just to get a crossbar to assist an outsider? Helping change a flat tire?

The best part was that these guys did not recognize me from my journalism exploits. To them, I was just a soul stuck on the side of the road. They would have made this stop for anyone.

My mind, a victim of big city upbringing, was blown.

If the existence of Floyd's Record Shop and Cajun Passover had me suspecting that I was in an alternate universe, then the actions of Officers Kevin Fontenot and Chip Matte provided absolute proof.

Without a dime in my pocket, there was no way I could thank these guys except by maybe a shout-out in one of my sports columns. In fact, I was determined to make my next column about the graciousness of this small town, along with my first impressions of Dr. Tim Fontenot (whom at this point I still never had a chance to chat with, as I could never catch up with the blur underneath the gold FDNY logo).

Fast-forward one year. Dr. Fontenot had buzzed the Daily World sports desk again. My editor informed me that the Big Daddy of Tee Cotton called and swore that NFL Films was going to cover TCB III for ESPN.

NFL Films? Tee Cotton? In the same sentence?

To say that the eyes of everyone in the Daily World sports department rolled like a riverboat slot machine would not do the scene justice. The message was taken with enough grains of salt to purge a crawfish pond.

Still, I made sure that Tee Cotton III was on my calendar.

The night before the game was a dinner to honor both schools. Out of curiosity and the hopes of a free meal, I slid in to Sacred Heart's gymnasium for the banquet. Alongside Dr. Tim and the coaches of both schools was a small gaggle of AV club alumni, looking like they'd just pulled off the biggest Radio Shack heist in history.

"Oh shoot," I cringed. "One just made eye contact with me."

The chieftain of their tribe came forward.

"Hi, I'm David Swain from NFL Films, and I have a couple of questions for you. Oh, and you'll have to sign a waiver in case we use you on television," the producer told me before pulling my year-old flat-tire sports column from his pocket.

NFL Films? Me? In the same sentence?

For a moment, I was floored.

Unfortunately, my flooring soon turned into the bottom falling out. Within weeks of TCB III and the accompanying NFL Films/ ESPN feature, my newspaper (under new ownership from Gannett – a huge corporation known affectionately in journalistic circles as the Death Star) decided to let me go for being too controversial and offensive in my sports columns.

I never did find a steady journalistic gig after that. Fortunately, I had enough of a reputation to keep busy by freelancing for other local publications. The Camaro was safe and I could still bum a free meal from a sports banquet or two.

Almost a year to the day of my bump from the Daily World, my sister and I were holed up in the Superdome to watch the Saints take on the Dallas Cowboys.

Actually, we were pretty much on top the 'Dome. Sis and I were perched in the Terrace level, home of cheap seats and mountain goats toting oxygen tanks. According to NASA, we were somewhere just south of the stratosphere, just north of the nachos kiosk. My kid sister and I managed the heights with a laugh as we swatted away passing weather balloons.

During the pregame, the P.A. announcer began describing what was happening back on the earth's surface. As Doris and I were comparing nosebleeds, I couldn't help but pick up a few words whispering in the echoes.

"*United Way... winner... Ville Platte... Tim Fontenot.*"

I did a double take towards the field. Squinting through a pair of freebie Sports Illustrated binoculars, I couldn't help but notice what was hiding behind an oversized check usually reserved for PGA accountants. It was the same smile which was usually hidden behind a blur of energy.

This time, the makeshift stage was under the goalposts to my left.

Wow. Just wow. There was Dr. Tim, collecting the *United Way Community Quarterback* award. With the nod came $10,000 he'd soon split between the rival schools he'd taken under his wing.

Little did I know that the brief ceremony held under the Saints' goalpost would mark the beginning of a much larger vision.

I lost touch with Tim in 2005, as I did pretty much with all reality. In May of that year, I was unexpectedly slammed with pancreatitis. A tea totaler in his mid 30's became riddled with the scarlet letter worn by elderly alcoholics. I'd been sucker-punched by fate.

I remember turning blue in a hospital bed, with a flurry of nurses freaking out and trying to locate a surgeon. I recall waking up two days later in ICU, with nothing better to do than count and recount the number of tubes and wires protruding from my body – all eighteen of them. I felt like a C-3PO unit flipped inside out.

Weeks in intensive care were followed by months on a feeding tube and a daily schedule that revolved around the *Price Is Right* and home health nurses (God help poor nurse Michelle if she interrupted Plinko). Sixteen surgeries in the next four years followed, along dozens of chance chronic attacks any time my internal organs wanted to relieve me of normalcy.

In my life, everything except the basics had to fall by the wayside. I could barely hold on to my day job as a schoolteacher due to excessive absences, much less string for the sports pages.

All my future freelance work as a sports reporter was shoved away for good. There was no way I could commit to a schedule with dirty ol' Panc and his random acts of flaring.

Four years after my life-changer, I was in my daily routine of scouring the Web for local news. At one site I tripped over a picture of some familiar faces. There was smilin' Tim Fontenot, along with Ville Platte coach Roy Serie, Sacred Heart coach Dutton Wall, and... Tony Dungy?

Yeah, that Tony Dungy.

Seemed the Tee Cotton Bowl story still made for a pretty good tale, as the photo was intended to reveal the winners of the *Win A Day Of Uncommon Service* contest held in 2009 by the legendary NFL coach/ best-selling author and his publisher, Tyndale House.

This must have been what it was like to see Shadrack, Mishack, and Abidnego hanging out with their fourth wheel. Riverboat slot machine eyes rolled again as I thought to myself, "How big is this little game going to get?"

Amazed, I had to find Tim and congratulate him. God and Google, of course, were asked to help me in this endeavor.

I soon located a good e-mail link to the good doctor. I sent him a typical 'Hey, how ya been' message.

Tim replied in a most gracious and enthusiastic way. I could almost see the grin through the screen.

He started telling me about Tee Cotton and Tony Dungy. Then, Tee Cotton and late college football/ pro wrestling standout Ernie 'Big Cat' Ladd. Then, Tee Cotton and parachute celebrations. Then, Tee Cotton and the Pope.

The Pope?

Yeah, that Pope.

Tim went on about his contacts all over the state, the nation, and the world that now knew of the Tee Cotton Bowl, and how the game had even been blessed by Pope John Paul II.

Dr. Tim invited me to his office and presented me with the letter of official Papal blessings on the game by the Vatican.

He revealed part of the 'care package' he would send out to draw attention to the game. That package included the column I wrote after Tee Cotton Bowl II, which referred to the town, the game, and the flat tire.

Wow. The sarcastic side of me thought, "What? I'm too controversial and offensive for the Opelousas *Daily World*, but not too controversial or offensive for the Pope?"

But I bit my tongue.

In the meantime, Tim mentioned that the rise of Tee Cotton would make for a good book.

I politely agreed.

He said, "No, I mean I want you to write the book. You're the guy."

I just shook my head, explained to him my illnesses and physical setbacks, and questioned my ability to donate the time needed to do the project justice. Four years after NG tubes, feeding tubes, art lines, main lines, drains and respirators, my pains were like my scars – somewhat faded, but still very much real and determined to become my permanent souvenirs.

Tim looked at me – smile gone for once – and said in all seriousness, "God uses broken people to do his will."

Great, just bring in the Big Guy into the equation.

Tim just grabbed me by the hands and we began to pray. Suddenly the best salesman in Louisiana prep sports signed me up with the ultimate Agent… an Agent that deals in broken things.

Things like me. Things like a flat tire.

CHAPTER ONE

Hakas, Hail Marys, and Hallelujahs

Top-tier NFL official Greg Gautreaux waits in the wings as he runs through some prepared words. A personal message from NBC analyst and former Super Bowl-winning coach Tony Dungy sits on a disc above a DVD player. Self-proclaimed 'Commissioner of Tailgating' Joe Cahn is leaving messages promising to be there, even though he's running late. Part of his tardiness is based on a weary flight from Los Angeles, where contract negotiations for a new television show were cut short so the *Commish* could make the night's event.

Dress rehearsal at the ESPY's in Hollywood, California, perhaps?

Nah.

It's only the roll call for the Tee Cotton Bowl banquet in Ville Platte, Louisiana.

Yes, Ville Platte, one of the numerous 'blink and you miss it' towns dotting the Pelican State's Acadian triangle, more affectionately known as Cajun country.

Tonight, three men used to packed stadiums holding 85,000 will find one way or another to appear at a sleepy little village of 8500. These football personalities, used to bright lights and worldwide media interests, now draw only the bulb of a local *Gazette* photographer.

Their attention is focused on a prep football city championship held between two small south Louisiana schools with records of little meaning in their 2A district, much less consequence of state or national concern.

But this is not any city championship or district game. This is the Tee Cotton (or *Small Cotton*) Bowl. Named after the town's Louisiana Cotton Festival, the TCB is a contest that over the past decade has garnered the attention of everyone from *NFL Films* to Pope John Paul II.

Clearly, there's something more at stake here than just a 'W' and an 'L'.

At 7:00 p.m., a small-framed man approaches the podium. Piercing brown eyes that hover under salt-peppered hair now peer out into the audience. Football players and cheerleaders from Sacred Heart High, an all-white Catholic school with around 250 high school students, are waltzing plates of sausage jambalaya to their tables. As they move and meander, they stop to co-mingle with their (technically speaking) cross-town rivals, the athletes of Ville Platte High – a school of 400,[1] with a seventy-seven percent African-American student population.

But stats concerning racial makeup are of little meaning to the students in attendance. At this banquet, the players from both teams are too excited to even notice school colors, much less skin colors. Besides, there is more important business to attend to – namely food and friendships.

The athletes in attendance are slow to move to the cafeteria tables. Members of the SHS Trojans and the VPH Bulldogs delay each other with playful banter. Like anyone born in south Louisiana, they know exactly how much talking

---

[1] Ville Platte High actually educates 5th-12th graders. Four-hundred represents the approximate number of 9th-12th graders at the school.

to engage in before the food grows cold. Tonight, these athletes are pushing their chitchat meters to the limits, as the small talk threatens to supercede suppertime.

There they were. Rivals. Shaking hands. Wishing each other well. Jockeying for position to sit *next* to their opponents for the dinner.

The scene is both the vision and reality for 'Doctor' Tim Fontenot, 53, a local physical therapist and football fanatic. Since 2000, he has molded the town's city championship into a phenomenon and the town's prep football fields into a mission field. It's moments like this that keep him going.

While 'Dr. Tim' may not be a household name to football fans in the vein of Cahn or Dungy, he is as much of a celebrity to tonight's crowd. Kids in the audience know that if it weren't for the free services Tim Fontenot and his colleagues provide for the athletes, a lot of them would not be able to afford to suit up, regulating their football dreams to backyards and *Madden*.

As Fontenot begins to speak, the crowd of predominately 13-18 year olds slides into silence, as if on cue.

The good doctor begins the banquet by giving a brief history of the Haka, the ceremonial Maori ritual performed by rugby rivals in New Zealand stadiums. Tim first became familiar with the tradition on a trip Down Under with his son, Jacob, in 2006. Fontenot instructs the teams of the deep, historic meaning of the chant. For tomorrow night's Tee Cotton Bowl pregame, seniors from both squads will be required to challenge each other by performing the war dance. It is an expected part of the TCB spectacle. For those seniors playing their last football game, it is also a rite of passage.

After the Haka hype, Dr. Tim talks about what he calls 'leading from behind'. He tells – almost commands – athletes from both schools to not just lead from example, but to lead by honoring those who played the game before them. He reminds them that people need an understanding of the city championship's rich history.

"You have people who have played this game that brought honor to your school," Dr. Tim allows the words to echo before continuing. "What are you going to do? What are you going to do this year to honor your name?"

Fontenot charges the athletes with the dare, much to the pleasure of alumni from the undefeated 1965 VPH Bulldog squad. The group of gentlemen, in for a reunion, quietly sit in a back corner of the cafeteria. Bonds of a small town run deep as athletes 45 years past their glory days have come in to check on their old stomping grounds.

Dr. Tim continues, "Last year's seniors wrote their name (in the bowl's history books). That was one of the greatest games I ever have seen, one of the most physical Tee Cotton Bowls I ever did see."

Just a half hour into the festivities, Fontenot begins to crank up the volume curiously early. His voice isn't reaching eleven yet, but it's definitely teetering on 10.5.

"Don't dishonor the game!"

The demand comes out of nowhere.

The intensity of his imperative takes everyone a bit by surprise. The shock occurs not because of the message but because of the messenger.

For fifty-one weeks out the year, the Tee Cotton creator is a textbook humbled Catholic gentleman – quiet and reverent in his every step, with the stealthy ability to disappear into any given crowd. But this is Tee Cotton Week, the week the founder gets to tap into his inner street preacher. The signal comes in loud and clear. Every word Dr. Tim now speaks attempts to one-up it's predecessor in volume and intensity.

"You have to be ready for your moment," Fontenot pushes. "Everyone here has a moment. Either your moment's going to pass you by, or you're going to grab it. It doesn't matter if it's short; if you grab it, it's yours and it will live forever."

With the last syllable, he turns on the monitor behind him. It's a clip of Super Bowl XLIII. More specifically, it's the fourth-quarter game-winning catch by the Pittsburgh Steelers' Santonio Holmes to put his team permanently ahead of the Arizona Cardinals, 27-23. The clip displays not only Holmes' athletic ability, but the aftermath. In that bowl game, an instant controversy arose as to if Holmes had one foot inbounds or two.

At that moment, a flurry of officials began to discuss the call and scour the instant replay booth.

"Millions of people were watching him to see if he was going to grab his moment or make a mistake. Santonio Holmes grabbed it," Dr. Tim said before taking the clip a bit deeper.

There's a slight pause before the host makes note of the official standing in back of the play, arms raised in confidence milliseconds after the catch.

That field judge was none other than Greg Gautreaux.[2] The eagle eyes that made the correct call in the biggest play of Super Bowl XLIII belonged to a local from

---

[2] *GO-trow*

Lafayette – the largest city in Cajun country, and a 40 minute drive south from the home of Tee Cotton.

More important than where Gautreaux was from, was where he was at, which was inside Sacred Heart's cafeteria and waiting for his introduction as guest speaker.

"In one-one hundreth of a second, he made the correct call that took five minutes and multiple camera views to prove right. (Greg) was ready for his moment," Fontenot said as the featured guest approached the podium.

By grabbing the microphone from Dr. Tim, Gautreaux joined a long line of distinguished Tee Cotton banquet speakers. Louisiana State University standout and former Cincinnati Bengal pro bowler Tommy Casanova – a one-time Sports Illustrated cover boy – made it to the mic in in a previous year. Grambling legend and pro wrestler (the late) Ernie 'Big Cat' Ladd was another big name to have spoken to this small room, as was Los Angeles Dodger Danny Ardoin.

Gautreaux used his opportunity to reminisce about his moment in the Super Bowl spotlight.

"It was an awesome experience, a great game," the field judge remembered. "The National Football League said that was probably the most physical Super Bowl they've seen played in the past 15 years. For a game like that to go down to the last minute and give you an opportunity to make the game-deciding call, and most importantly to get it right, I can't tell you how much of an awesome experience that was."

From there, the guest hopped into his message of competitiveness to the two high school teams already steeped in the meaning.

"Competition is something you're going to use in your life everyday. You're going to be competing with your friends for a job. There's competition in test scores. All that is competition. Get used to that for the rest of your life."

The keynote speaker continued by giving a brief history of how he worked his way from a mere playground referee at the Lafayette Parks and Recreation Department all the way to an official on sport's biggest stage.

Having gone from rec ball to prep, prep to college, college to college bowls, and then ultimately to the NFL and the Super Bowl, the speaker attributed his success to setting – and then achieving – goals.

"I put an application into the NFL. What have I got to lose?"

Once he was in the big leagues, Gautreaux admits he started daydreaming.

"What about officiating playoffs.... playoffs... *PLAYOFFS?*"

The thought, done in his best Jim Mora impression, takes in a bit of explosive laughter from the student-athletes.

Gautreaux the goal-setter did eventually get his wish to supervise NFL playoff games, including the infamous Blizzard Bowl between the New Orleans Saints and the Chicago Bears at Soldier Field for the 2006 season's NFC Championship.

After the crowd dies down, the guest speaker turns the topic from the Super Bowl to Tee Cotton to life itself. He starts quizzing his audience.

"Right now you're playing as a team and setting goals as a team, but later on in life, you're going to be alone. How are you going to set your goals? How are you going to attain them?"

With the young audience still picking at remnants of sausage and rice, Gautreaux feeds them his own recipe for success: choices, attention to detail, and faith.

"The choices you make in life are going to dictate where you go in life," he instructs. "You make choices every day, every minute. You can follow a path by where you want to go with your choices."

Gautreaux goes on to explain how attention to detail allowed him to make a decision in the blink of an eye.

"I got that call right at the Super Bowl because everything I did over the years in officiating helped me get the call right that time. I had the right mechanics, the concentration. My focus was there.

"How do you concentrate in a game where you have 75,000 people in the stands cheering? Everything around you says 'Super Bowl'. You've got a team that's going to win and a team that's going to lose. You've got to make that decision. How do you concentrate on that?

"It takes discipline."

At that point, the keynote speaker then begins to slide to his last talking point – faith.

The forthcoming topic shocks absolutely no one in attendance.

Faith and football are not two competing, or even complementing, themes for Tee Cotton Week. Dr. Tim's vision requires that faith and football, for five days, become one in the same. Together, they form a singular strong cloth that holds the community together. It is the bold weaving of the two that quite possibly has allowed Tee Cotton to garner attention from places far away from the average Ville Platte resident's *TomTom*.

Because of the intensive faith-football connection inherent in Dr. Tim's plan, the night's banquet – as all past Tee Cotton banquets – occurs on the campus of Sacred Heart Catholic. While participation is voluntary on the part of VPH's public school athletes, the Bulldog nation tonight is 100% in attendance.

Gautreaux, like the guest speakers to come in previous years, sees no need to edit himself. A devout believer, Gautreaux has the green light to discuss whatever comes naturally.

"The third area I want to talk about – and the most important – is having strong faith and belief as a Christian," Gautreaux says as he brings his keynote to it's final act. He discusses the pillars of his Christian and Catholic beliefs in a soft timbre, in contrast to Dr. Tim's unbridled tones.

"That has so much to do with your life," mentions the ref. "When you become a Christian person and you are a Christian person, you learn what respect is. You'll feel respect, and you will show respect."

Gautreaux then segues into bullet points on integrity, sportsmanship, and compassion before driving home the power of prayer.

"Guys – and ladies that are here – I can't tell you how powerful the power of The Lord's Prayer can be in your life. One of the things in the NFL I did not like was that I could not attend Mass on Sundays. I couldn't do it because of the schedule and requirements. Very seldom could I make a Mass on Sunday. So what I did was make weekday Mass from Mondays through Fridays. I figured five-to-one was not a bad deal. I've been doing that for eight years.

"I know the power of prayer is so important. Each weekday in the morning, I start off my day with a physical routine and a spiritual routine. At 5:30 in the morning, I'm in the streets running. I'll run three and-a-half miles each day. While I am running, I'll pray the Rosary. I ask the Lord to help me. Give me the courage, the confidence, the strength. Help me focus and concentrate. All the things that I do, I ask the Lord to help me. I've been doing this for a while and I really believe that's what helped me to get to the Super Bowl after all these years – it's the power of prayer."

He closes with one last question to the football players, cheerleaders, and invited guests before winding down his speech.

"We prepare ourselves for athletic contests every day, but do we spiritually prepare for the conflicts that we face each day of our lives?"

After a few polite anecdotes on Brett Farve and the Army-Navy game (which Gautreaux was a part of in his

NCAA officiating days), the microphone is relayed back to the host.

Dr. Tim uses the opportunity to honor members of the Ville Platte High 1965 football team in attendance. He then runs a short clip on NFL Hall-Of-Famers before once again dialing up his inner evangelist.

"What God gave us here is a gift," the founder addresses to the crowd. "Are we going to throw it to the sky and say 'Thank You!' and make the most of it?"

He then tells the attendees about a much-appreciated miracle that has aided his vision over time – the growing number of volunteers that come out annually just to make sure the the town has it's best face forward during Tee Cotton Week.

"Last year, people just started showing up and painting goalposts!" the founder exclaims in gracious excitement.

Over the years, the Tee Cotton Bowl has had it's share of help. Scout troops are known to place American flags on the field; over a dozen churches of every denomination act as prayer partners; an army of fathers make up the 'Cracked' pyrotechnic team that help set off thousands of dollars in pre-game fireworks.

Once Tim finishes recognizing the hard work put forth by the community for its shining moment, his piercing eyes once again begin to scan the audience. The host's countenance makes a change.

It's not like he'd found a new gear. It's more like the Tee Cotton creator had found a new engine.

With his second wind, Dr. Tim starts marching table-to-table.

"All He wants is everything we got. Every ounce of you. Can you do that?"

Now, the knob is up to 11.

Like Q*Bert with Ritalin withdrawals, Dr. Tim hops from group-to-group, where many students are sitting in various mixes of black-and-white, Sacred Heart and Ville Platte High.

"Can you do that?" he repeats the refrain as he moves from one table to the next. "Can you do that?

"There are boys that would love to play tomorrow. Jacob Fontenot,[3] senior year, last game. He's injured. Can you play for him? He'd love to play; he'd give anything to play! Can you play for him?"

---

[3] Not Tim's son, but another with the popular local surname. Fontenot families take up an incredible five pages worth of phone book space in the small town directory.

With the dare, he also instructs: "You can't let the guy across from you quit!"

If the Tee Cotton creator has an unwavering demand, it's for an athlete to give his opponent the best he can, to ensure the other player is forced to give the best he's got in return.

It is a football philosophy not from a playbook but from the Good Book. Tim's gridiron values come from Proverbs 27:17.[4]

"The harder he plays, the better you've got to be," Tim translates the verse into something more athlete-friendly. "That's a challenge. You think that Mamou (another area high school) could handle that? Pine Prarie (High School)? They don't understand what this game is about!"

Dr. Tim begins to tear through the crowd like a buzz saw.

"God can make you better by playing football. If you give Him everything you've got, He won't ask for anything more. Can you do that? Can you pick up and do that?"

With that statement, the loom that weaves Tee Cotton's faith-and-football cloth pops into overdrive.

In the crowd of blue-and-gold Sacred Heart jerseys and purple-and-white Ville Platte High uniforms stands a

---

[4] "As iron sharpens iron, so man sharpens his fellow man." (NAB)

man who's skin is now literally turning red with intensity. This man has sacrificed his microphone as the words demand *he* speak them at full volume. Electrical amplification need not apply.

"It's a special game. God blessed it. This is a gift from God. Our gift, what we give back, is how we play tomorrow."

Taking a break to catch his breath, Dr. Tim uses a video about football and race in South Carolina to drive his point home.

"Don't let fear get in our way," the TCB founder tells the teams after the clip, this time going back to the microphone and a much calmer tone. "We don't care if someone is Baptist or Catholic or Black or White – we're all Christian beings. We do this to bring the community together. We play this high school game the way nobody else plays."

Once again, the finger that is on the pulse of the community now hits the 'play' button on the DVD player. This time, Tony Dungy appears.

Coach Dungy is of particular importance to tonight's event. The past spring, both Ville Platte High head coach Roy Serie and Sacred Heart coach Dutton Wall, along with Dr. Tim and his son, had an opportunity to meet with the legend as part of the prize for winning the *Win A Day Of Uncommon Service with Tony Dungy* contest sponsored by Dungy's publisher, Tyndale House.

The clip is a personal one, especially recorded for the event. Like a kinder, gentler Max Headroom, the bust inside the television seems to come alive in it's own way.

"I'm very sorry I couldn't be there tonight," Mr. Dungy apologizes via the DVD player. "Even though I can't be there, I want you to know that it's an honor for me to share a few words with you before the big game tomorrow. It's more than a game. It's a chance for you to make a statement about yourself as a player, as a competitor, and ultimately about yourself as a man."

Dungy's down-to-earth tones bring a certain hush to the room.

"You want to be on the winning team, but understand that victory is what you all want as you sit together tonight and share a meal, as you fellowship and recognize one another's strengths.

"Because you've chosen to be an athlete, you've also chosen to be a leader and a role model. Others look up to you whether you realize or not. Young athletes on your campus and in your community look at you as an example. Who are you modeling?

"I want to encourage you guys to model Jesus Christ. You can do it. I John 4:4 says this – the One who is in you is greater than the one within the world.

"You can stand up. With the power of the Holy Spirit living within you, you can overcome, you can stand out and you can say 'no' to the temptations of the world.

"No matter what the outcome of the game is going to be, the bigger outcome has already been recorded into the record books. Tomorrow, you'll have an opportunity to show everyone who is watching – and yourselves – what Christianity is all about."

There is a slight silence after the monitor is turned off. Dr. Tim, in his role of emcee, looks for signs that Dungy's words have settled in.

The long list of speeches and clips over with, and empty Styrofoam shells being bused from tables, Fontenot has just one last piece of unfinished business before dismissal.

Haka practice.

A huddle of seniors from both squads find a spare corner in the back of the Sacred Heart cafeteria. In the center of this mass of humanity, of course, is Dr. Tim.

Fontenot's head pops up from the middle of the pile. The good doctor begins screaming, except this time, the tone has gone from tent revivalist to field general.

"*Ka mate! Ka mate! Ka ora! Ka ora!*" he leads, shouting words that make up the aboriginal war cry, *'I die! I die! I live! I live!'*

"*Ka mate! Ka mate! Ka ora! Ka ora!*" team members from both sides echo.

For the older adults in attendance, it's a long way from '*Laissez Le Bon Temp Rouler.*'

The chorus continues until a final "*A upane kaupane whiti te ra! Hi!*" (*Up to the top the sun shines!*) is yelled. At the end of the chant, athletes from both schools jump up and down, smiling and high-fiving each other.

Wasn't this supposed to be a war cry?

Tim busily gives final instructions to the teams for the next night's contest. As he is going over the to-do list, attention is unexpectedly drawn to a figure entering the doors on the other side of the building. The apparition is a perfectly-timed arrival, like a *deus ex machina* on a cheesy made-for-tv movie. Except this is no film star. It's a loud-talking New Orleans native. Tufts of white beard hair protrude like a tazed bag of cotton balls. No fancy Hollywood wardrobe, the balding man dons only a white t-shirt, a pair of rolled-up jeans, and sneakers. Partially hidden behind the cotton-ball beard is a smile that looks ready to explode with a thousand tales simultaneously.

The fashionably late arrival is none other than 'Tailgating Commissioner' Joe Cahn.

The same crowd of high school football players that just smothered Dr. Tim during Haka practice now give Mr. Cahn the same warm rush.

"I'd just like to say how blessed you have made me and how I've talked about you around the country," the *Commish* announces in a typical Crescent City drawl, somewhat distinct in a room of Cajun accents.

One of the Cahn's thousand tales launches from behind the beard.

"Over the past 14 years, I've done over 500 games, travelled 500,000 miles. This week, something special has taken place. I got a call from a network, and they said to me, 'We'd like to talk tailgating; we're thinking about a tailgating show.'

"This happened a week ago.

"They said, 'We'd like to talk to you.'

"I said, 'Well right now, I'm in Dallas.' Last week I was with TCU on Saturday, in Dallas on Sunday, was going to New Orleans on Monday night.

"They said, 'can we come and see?'

"I said, 'Yes you can come and see. What you see is what you get.'

"So they came in, and it wasn't really much of a meeting. It was to be their people talking to my people, but I don't have any people," Cahn drops to surrounding laughter, "so I had to talk to them.

"We had a nice meeting, and they said 'We're thinking about a tailgating show, and we'd like to sign you to a 'free agency.'

"I'm all for it.

"This Monday, I get an e-mail. It said, 'Can you come out to Los Angeles on Wednesday.'

"I said 'No.'

"They said, 'What do you mean, 'No?'

"I said, 'I'm going to the Tee Cotton Bowl.'

"They said, 'Wait a minute, we're *XYZ !*... and I can't tell you right now who it is because of a confidentiality clause due to my agent."[5]

Cahn pauses with a smile that emerges slightly from the tazed-cotton ball beard.

"Actually, I don't have an agent," he tells the huddle. "I just said that to impress you."

---

[5] The network later turns out to be TLC; the show, *Tailgating Taketown.*

A group of students worn from one long day and facing another in the morning are too busy laughing with the gentleman to worry about sleep.

"So I said to them, 'I can't come, I'm going to the Tee Cotton Bowl. That's in Ville Platte.

"He said, 'Wait a minute. We're offering you a contract, and to fly you out to Los Angeles, and you're going where? *Village Plattey*?

"No, Ville Platte.

"So they said, 'Can you come on Thursday?'

"I said, 'No, that's the game... Wednesday's the banquet.[6] Now I had the dates a little mixed up. That's why its important in school to learn math, so you can learn what what day it is."

The commissioner's quip keeps the giggles going.

"I said, 'I can't come'

"So they said (on Monday), can you come tomorrow? I said, 'Yes, I'm not doing anything on Tuesday. I can come out to Los Angeles. But I've got to be back!'

"They said, 'Okay, we'll just fly you here and fly you back.'

"4 1/2 hours there; 4 1/2 hours back.

---

[6] Actually, the TCB banquet occurred on Thursday, November 5, 2009; Tee Cotton X rolled on Friday, November 6th.

"I go to the their headquarters, and man, I am impressed. But they don't have any food there, so I'm not that impressed. Nice chairs and tables and computers, but where's the food?

"So we sat down with the national director of programming, the head of the West Coast feed and the head of the East Coast feed. And they kept saying, 'The East Coast feed' and I kept saying 'Feed? Feed! That's right, I need food!'"

More laughter comes from the amassed huddle at the man who makes his living scouring parking lots for eats.

Finally, Cahn's tale, wandering like the Mississippi River, makes it's way to it's final point, a point that means everything to those in the semi-circle.

"But by seeing your faces, I want to let you know it was more important for me to be out here than to be out there, because what you stand for is so very important to this country.

"Last year, I talked about the Army-Navy game. Then after the game, I asked everybody to watch each other's back. You are all neighbors. One neighbor can call up another neighbor and say, 'My house is on fire! Can you come and help me?' And you wouldn't say, 'What school did you go to?' You're all part of Ville Platte."

"And that's my message that I tell, that you are carrying to the rest of the country. We have our differences. We're always going to have our differences, especially those of you that are thin... but there is hope for you," the pudgy Cahn riffs with a sly wink.

The Commish dismisses the group with one last reason to smile.

"What we are doing is trying to say that what is being accomplished here in Ville Platte – with Dr. Fontenot and everybody, the coaches and everybody – well, this is one of the most amazing events in the country. I just wanted to come out here and salute you. I just wanted to say that you guys are my heroes. You guys are showing that it can work."

After the final gracious compliment, Cahn heads towards his RV, which will rest for the night at Ville Platte High's stadium. Some students hang around the cafeteria, but most head home knowing the importance of rest before the big day.

One person still bopping around unrepentantly, his adrenaline level not about to surrender, is Dr. Tim.

Tonight, he is the kid on Christmas Eve.

CHAPTER TWO

A Busy Day for the Good Doctor

It's a bit past 8 o'clock on a crisp Friday morning in November. The sleepy town of Ville Platte is just waking itself up to the sounds of KVPI's bilingual news program, *La Tasse de Café ('A Cup of Coffee')*. Informational tidbits are being read in both English and the colloquial Cajun French by host Charlie Manuel.

His soothing, deep monotone is sliced with a Ginsu, however, as he fields a phone call from one Jennifer Vidrine.

As if the town didn't have enough reminders that today was D-Day (or rather, Tee-Day), Ms. Vidrine, a disco-era Ville Platte High homecoming queen and community activist, begins a long line of friendly challenges and wagers between the alumni from her school and that of the Sacred Heart Trojans. Her voice has all the energy of an IV needle hooked up to an espresso press. She talks in enthusiastic bursts that melt snooze buttons all over Evangeline Parish.

Meanwhile, at an intersection roughly two miles away from Ville Platte High, soaking in the radio waves and reveling in the pre-game chatter is Tee Cotton founder Tim Fontenot. He is busy leading a two-truck convoy to the school's stadium.

Following behind Dr. Tim's Chevy Suburban is Clarence LaFleur. Mr. LaFleur's pickup is weighed down with a boatload of tents, tables, chairs, and other accessories being hauled for a day's worth of tailgating.

In Tim's vehicle is his son, Jacob, 26, clutching a Cajun treasure more precious than gold.

Boudin.[7]

The aroma of the rice and pork-based treat fills the cabin of the old vehicle. For a Cajun like Fontenot, the mere fumes from the box act like a Louisiana version of Red Bull.

This is a good thing, as the Tee Cotton's founder will need all the energy he can muster today. Already up for five

---

[7] *BOO-dahn* – actually a sausage, although a sacrilege to refer to it as such in Cajun country

hours, Dr. Tim began his day at 3 a.m. when he awoke early enough to fix lunch for his wife, Suzy. A physical therapist like her husband, Suzy has a long – if less glamorous – day in front of her as well. While Tim will be making media rounds, she will be making home-health rounds. Later in the day, as Tim makes double-checks at the stadium, she will be charting at a local nursing home.

With her lunch made, the good doctor took off to 6:30 a.m. mass at Sacred Heart Church and then a run at B&S Market for the good eats at hand.

Next on Dr. Tim's agenda is to wake up a certain soon-to-be television celebrity for a trip to the local radio station.

At long last, the Suburban and the tag-along pickup pull behind the north end goalpost of Ville Platte High's football stadium, surrounding the R.V. of one Joe Cahn.

Tim exits his vehicle wearing a specially designed half-purple/half-blue T-shirt that commemorates the town's two high schools.

Swiftly, he sprints to the RV's door, knocking loudly to wake up the Commish.

Too late. The tailgating king, already raring to go, swings open the door with a grin and a proudly-displayed iPhone.

"I just updated my Facebook," Cahn says as he shows everyone the photo of a freshly killed pig that will be the focus of today's early-morning *boucherie*.[8]

"Tee Cotton Bowl is the game of the week," Joe reads the website update from his phone. "Tailgating begins with a boucherie. Squirrel sauce piquant[9] will be ready shortly. Sixty-eight and sunny."

After Joe's proclamation, Dr. Tim bears an offering of the boudin to his guest.

"Breakfast of champions," Fontenot jokes.

Cahn trades a sample for another one of his stories.

"Last night, I asked Coach (Roy Serie of VPH) if I had the urge, at midnight, if I could take my ball and run 100 yards for a touchdown. The coach said, 'Well, yes."

"I told him, 'I didn't say, 'May I?' I said, 'Could I?'"

Cahn went on to describe the attempt in comedic bravado, only to end his story in disappointment when "my knee touched before I could reach the pylon."

The Commissioner keeps the mood light. Meanwhile, his constant travel partner – a tabby cat named Sophia – sits in the driver's chair and stares quietly out the window. Although silent, she wears an expression that says,

---

[8] *BOO-shuh-REE*
[9] *pe-KAHNT*

"Fine. Don't offer me boudin. They'll be a gift waiting on this seat later."

Tim busies himself by chatting with some early-morning volunteers and devising the day's game plan. At the same time, Joe's thoughts switch to the spicy impromptu breakfast. It seems difficult for Cahn to take a bite without offering a bit of gastronomic philosophy.

"We like peppery hot food for several reasons," the top tailgater explains to those around him. "Number one, it stimulates the taste buds. It lets you know that your mouth is alive. It knows that you are chewing something. But more than that, there's the chemical Capsaicin, which is an endorphin stimulant. Basically, people get high eating (spicy) hot food. It puts you on a different level."

Capsaicin could explain why Dr. Fontenot is pinballing around the stadium five hours after waking the owls.

Tim's bounce is stopped momentarily by one of the trillions of phone calls he will field that day. On the other end of the cell is VPH principal Kelli Lafleur. The good doctor pleads with her to delay the boucherie crew. He needs them to hit the pause button on the cooking process for 30 minutes so he and Joe Cahn can run to *La Tasse* for a quick interview.

Able to buy an extra half hour from the principal, Tim sweeps into southern gentleman mode.

Instead of a quick "Thanks" and "Bye", he closes the conversation with "You're *awesome*. You're one of my dream principals."

After hanging up the phone, Tim explains that "These two young ladies (Ms. Lafleur of VPH and Dawn Shipp, assistant principal of Sacred Heart in charge of the high school wing, both in their first year) have really been active. They believe in this. It makes what I do a lot easier."

Tim, Jacob, and Joe hop in Fontenot's SUV for their morning interview. Not three minutes out the gate, like a police dog trained to sniff out cayenne instead of cocaine, Cahn zooms in on Café de Lasalle, one of the many hole-in-the-wall eateries around town that they pass. Immediately, he begins to drill Tim for more information.

Tim shares an impromptu review, stating, "This is good! In fact, they are doing the fried fish and gumbo for the Southern drum line."

Southern, as in the collegiate Bayou Classic band with five Super Bowl appearances to their credit. This football season, Southern University will ultimately perform at the NFC Championship game between the New Orleans Saints and the Minnesota Vikings. But first, the Jaguar percussionists – also known as the Heartbeat of the Human Jukebox – are making a pit stop in Cajun country for Tee Cotton X.

Their appearance tonight, while special, is not surprising. There is a tight connection between the Ville Platte community and the institutions of Southern University of Baton Rouge and McNeese State of Lake Charles. Even though there are colleges closer geographically to the town, none are closer to the heart than the Jaguars and the Cowboys. Each is about an hour's drive southeast or southwest of the town, respectively.

"The thing about it is," Jacob Fontenot notes, "both schools we kind of have ties with. The A.D. from Southern (Greg Lafleur) is from Ville Platte High. With me and my dad's ties to McNeese, we kind of do the back door, 'Hey, can you do this for us?'"

The Fontenots are born-and-bred MSU Cowboys. Jacob studies forensics there; Dr. Tim, an alumnus, still works the sidelines as a trainer during football season.

"A lot of people do stuff for free, especially if they're from Ville Platte," explains the younger Fontenot. "It never hurts to ask, and if you ask nicely, they're more than willing to come. It makes it fun."

For tonight, Tim must have asked Lafleur really nice – *pretty please with sugar on top* nice – as he had no problem borrowing the famed drum line.

But SU's arrival is seven hours away. Right now Tim is more worried about the pending on-air interview. Entering KVPI studio's radio booth, he cradles his box of breakfast goodies like Paris clutching her Chihuahua. Following right behind are Jacob and Joe.

They enter the room stealthily while local radio personality Charlie Manuel reads the news in French. As the Tee Cotton crew slips in, Manuel changes his voice inflection from morning monotone to something more welcoming and boisterous. Still using a blur of French, the only word that could be deciphered by a non-Cajun listener is, of course, 'boudin.'

Surrounded in the booth by autographed black-and-white promo photos of the musicians of yesteryear – artists such as Dottie West, Eddie Raven, and the Beach Boys – Charlie switches to a few words of English before the commercial break.

"Hey Tim, you think that the Ville Platte bear is here?"

Charlie refers to a stray black bear that made its way to a Ville Platte neighborhood in June. The animal was practically a local celebrity the past summer, and Tim's been promising the townsfolk a return visit for the game.

The good doctor knocks on the table.

"He's at the door!"

For a decade Tim has been successfully coaxing everyone from NFL Films to the Tailgating Commissioner to make it to the city's championship. Because of his previous guest lists, no one in the room is quite sure if Tim is joking or not about the bruin's potential cameo. Maybe the founder's newest self-inflicted dare was to sweet-talk those outside of his own species to come attend.

With Tim, no one ever really knows.

Charlie, in a resonant voice, responds to the knock. "I don't trust Tim anymore than I trust Jennifer," he says in reference to Ms. Vidrine's earlier call.

During the commercial break, the box of boudin makes its way around the room. It seems more than just a snack; the food is more like an alternate form of currency. After witnessing the reverence in which the treat is handled, one can just imagine someone driving to a Ville Platte car dealership with a refrigerator truck full of the stuff, and trading the contents for a new dually diesel.

Tim takes a very short turn at the microphone before attention is drawn to the Tailgating Commissioner. Cahn continues his transformation from comedian to philosopher, describing to the station's listeners what it's like to view Ville Platte from the outside in.

"I've got to tell you one thing. Being from New Orleans and coming out to Cajun country is such a pleasure," he compliments. "The traditions maintain, even the radio stations maintain out here. We're losing that in this country. As I travelled around, starting in 1996, I went to every stadium in the NFL in one season. Since then, I've been to over 500 games; 500,000 miles, and what you have in this country – and it's really sad – in every corner, you see the same thing. You see the same businesses, whether or not you travel from Seattle to Miami, if you're traveling from New England to San Diego. It's generic, except here in south Louisiana – especially here in Ville Platte. That's why I came back."

Ville Platte's big guest of honor, on his second trip to the TCB, continues a few more observations about *'Bow-Deen'*, jokingly mispronouncing the local snack. He marvels at the Cajun art of eating the slippery sausage while driving and how Cajuns are 'going green' by licking their fingers clean instead of wasting paper towels on the wash-up task.

Joe Cahn begins wrapping up his turn at the microphone by giving his own predictions as to where the bear might be.

"I'm going to say the bear is not afraid of jumping out of the plane. That bear walked over to Ville Platte High and saw the pig. Now the pig, he'd been stuck. He's hanging up by his legs.

"That's what happened to the bear. He doesn't know that 'boucherie' means pig; it doesn't mean bear. But be that as it may..."

Cahn leaves the air chair with one final piece of praise to the town.

"There are people out there that are just existing. They get up in the morning; they go to sleep at night. There's no laughs. But here (in Ville Platte), people are still living. They're living the good life. There may not be a Mercedes, but I tell you, the riches of this town are in its children, its citizens, and its culture."

Joe switches places with Tim. The radio conversation finally turns away from boudin and bruins, as Fontenot gives a compliment to the Ultimate Tee Cotton Fan.

"You know how we've all been praying and fasting for the game?" Tim reminds the listeners of radio and print ads he'd put out with the request. "Well, Jesus has blessed us. God not only multiplies loaves and fish. I've been getting so many calls of people wanting to donate pigs (for the boucherie), it's almost like he can multiply hogs, too."

Judging from the amount of hands that have been in the boudin box already this morning, apparently the good Lord had also done some quick exponential calculations with the day's brunch.

The morning host gives Tim a quick reminder of Jennifer Vidrine's earlier wager.

"Tim, I don't know if you know this, but Jennifer called a little earlier. She was telling us that Ville Platte High will bring that trophy back home. She says she has twelve bets already."

Tim Fontenot, a Sacred Heart graduate himself, doesn't take the bait.

"I have to be very Solomon-like in my judgment. I'm going to make a prediction. I predict that whoever comes out will have fun, and the game will be a *Thrilla in the Villa*."

While remaining neutral down to his Tee shirt, Tim does remind the radio station that his friends don't have to follow the same guidelines. He notes, "I've got some Sacred Heart people that'll stand up to her.

"I'm not going to be in on this. I've got to walk the line. We're just going to see who plays better that night. After, we're going to hug both teams and say, 'Good job.'"

"You just want to be the promoter?" the host asks, while listeners ponder how much neutral Swiss blood must flow through the good doctor's veins.

"I just want to see the kids play hard and play clean," Tim answers. "After that, we'll just give all the glory to God. And guess what? You can't outgive him."

With that remark, the radio host turns back to his microphone and begins another turbo-charged French soliloquy.

A befuddled Cahn, not being able to translate the Cajun dialect, drops another one-liner in the background.

"As they say in New Orleans, '*Yeah, you right!*'"

The trio of Tim, Jacob, and Joe head back to Ville Platte High stadium; it is now 8:55 a.m. Besides the boucherie going on in the north end zone – an official part of the tailgating agenda – a small tent has popped up just outside the south gates. Some Ville Platte High supporters have unloaded their barbeque pit to make their claim as the first fans at the stadium, ten hours before kickoff.

"When you come out and see this, it really pumps you up," Dr. Tim says as he watches the family set up.

By the ticket booth, a slaughtered pig is hanging upside-down from a farm tractor's winch. Its head is wedged in an ice chest to gather remaining drops of blood. Nearby, Joe and Tim are milling about a half-dozen cooks and volunteers. They are mostly retirement-aged folk, born at a time when such a cookout was done not for celebration, but for survival. They were raised in an era when Cajuns would cut up a whole hog as meals for winter, rather than a picnic for a day.

The situation endears itself to the Commissioner.

"It's one of those great cultural situations that we're losing," Cahn waxes. "Instead of having three, four, five families together to do a boucherie for their families' provisions, you now go to the store. You run to the store and get a lottery ticket and get a plastic bag full of something. That's sad."

While the old folks are busy prepping the pig, some of the older men are getting the *Cajun Microwave* ready. They are preparing coals to go on the lid of the cast-iron hotbox smoker.

Someone in the background looks at the pig and shouts, "Sexy!"

Being in the middle of Cajun country and knowing the vast variety of meals an Acadian native could do with such a hog, one cannot be sure the comment was meant to be a bit of sarcasm and not a legitimate compliment.

Just a few feet away, a pickup truck's trailer serves as a makeshift stage as the Ville Platte Playboys[10] tune up for Tee Cotton's morning concert.

The concert is one of two scheduled for the day. Closer to showtime, JJ and the Zydeco Dog Pound will be performing on the field, representing Cajun music's more rhythm-and-blues oriented cousin.

Jacob is engaged in conversation with some others observing the morning cookout when suddenly he is interrupted by a spry and elderly gentleman. It is none other than Fox, the leader of the aforementioned Playboys. The grey-haired singer is decked out in a cowboy hat, sunglasses, and a western shirt adorned with American flag patches. He breaks the ice the way many people do in this area – with a handful of 'Boudreaux and Thibodeaux' jokes popular in Cajun country.

The musician rattles off three such anecdotes in succession. The first Fox tale concerns Boudreaux's

---

[10] Music lovers outside of Acadiana can be assured the band, regardless of the name, is family-friendly. The term *Playboys* is not a nod to Hugh Hefner's hedonistic empire, but the nomenclature given to many traditional Cajun bands in the area. Every town in the Acadiana triangle usually has at least one local Cajun band, and that band is usually named 'The (*name of town*) Playboys.'

encounter with a Kung Fu master. The next describes a road trip to Georgia for the hapless Cajun and his friend Thibodeaux, and their subsequent misinterpretations of road signs they come upon.

The final Boudreaux and Thibodeaux adventure Fox explains concerns a two-dollar chicken.

It is a joke best not repeated in mixed company.

With the younger Fontenot in stitches, Fox disappears as quickly as he'd arrived.

After he leaves, Jacob focuses on the boucherie crew, who are now dividing the slaughtered pig into smaller parts. Meanwhile, Joe Cahn has now totally transformed himself from jester into a serious student of food prep. He documents the crew's every movement with a digital still camera as well as a video camera.

At 9:30 a.m., reinforcements arrive. An SUV barrels in close behind the theater of operations, towing a huge smoker of at least 10 feet in length.

The *Cajun Microwave* is now on autopilot, adding further momentum to the cause.

A group of young and curious schoolchildren led by their teacher come out to watch. One of the volunteers couldn't help but have a little fun. She pulls a glob of intestines the size of a basketball and asks, "Ya'll like boudin? This is where it comes from!"

There's that *b* word again.

Joe Cahn points and says, "Hey kids, if you don't smoke, your lungs will look like that!"

Missing the twisted observations are Tim and Jacob, who are too busy carrying a bunch of New Orleans Saints flags to the field.

Tim stops just long enough to greet Phil Veillon, who is manning a blue tent under the end zone. Veillon, a 1979 Ville Platte High graduate, has been charged with the honor of preparing a squirrel sauce piquant for the Commish.

The hunter begins by pulling some cleaned squirrel carcasses from a Ziploc bag. For good measure and good taste, a few thumb-sized pieces are tossed into the pot. Closer observation allows one to see these meaty flavor nuggets have eye sockets.

In the stew goes squirrel heads.

As hunting tales are tossed around like war stories, Cahn briefly switches back to comedian mode.

"I think that hunting (squirrels) with a .22 is kind of savage. I like to do it with a slingshot. To tell you the truth, darts. Nah – blowguns. I learned that from the Pygmies. (I can) hit a squirrel at 900 yards as it flies through the air."

The small group, huddled around the pot and defeated as to know how to top Cahn's silliness, gets back to the silent task of inhaling the onions and spices that make up the roux.

Around 10:30 a.m., the field begins to take shape. The Tee-Tron arrives.

Leave it up to Cajun ingenuity to come up with a big screen for their big game. In this case, the Tee-Tron 'big screen' is a huge sheet covering the entire side panel of the box of a moving van. Combined with a projector, it will be used to run footage of Tee Cotton Hall of Famers and prior Tee Cotton highlights come game time.

Next to the Tee-Tron (itself looking like a prop in a Boudreaux-and-Thibodeaux punch line), an American flag flies at half-mast. In the midst of all the celebration, there is need for remembrance of the massacre of American soldiers in Fort Hood, Texas a day earlier.

Huge banners at least eight feet in length flank both entrances of the stadium. Each bolt is screen-printed with a huge photograph of previous Tee Cotton memories. In the middle of the field is a 25-foot wide insignia created in both teams' colors.

On this clear blue day, a slight wind tasks itself with carrying the opening notes of the morning's entertainment.

Fox is bobbing up and down on stage like a broken member of the Whack-A-Mole community. The music is too infectious not to want to tap along to.

While the Ville Platte Playboys provide a suitable soundtrack, Tim continues setting up Saints-themed displays to go alongside the Sacred Heart and VPH items.

Flags, inflatable helmets, and ballooning cartoon player replicas all begin to go up in response to the team's historic season.

Dr. Tim, an unrepentant New Orleans fan, shows a bit of pride when asked why he's putting up pro football displays for a high school game that's a three-hour drive away from the Superdome.

"I buy a lot of Saints stuff, so I put it out. That's one of my perks; I can do what I want. It's very appropriate."

Appropriate, indeed, as the New Orleans Saints are in the midst of their first Super Bowl campaign. Today, the pro team is *the* water cooler topic around the state. In fact, Tee Cotton X Week kicked off for both teams with the schools coming down with *Who Dat* fever. Besides a flagpole prayer in the morning, the other agenda item on the Monday of TCB Week was a nighttime weenie roast for seniors from both high schools, where together they watched the Saints'

35-27 drubbing of the Atlanta Falcons on Monday Night Football.

To hear Dr. Tim talk about his beloved favorite NFL team is to hear – perhaps for the only time – him being a bit arrogant. But whatever words he says in pride about the Saints this morning will be atoned for tonight. One of the giveaways being held during the game will be tickets for an upcoming Saints home stand against Tampa Bay. The passes are sacrificed straight from Dr. Tim's personal season ticket stash.

After his Saintly thoughts, Tim goes back to the business of laying out a labyrinth of power cords – cords for inflatables; cords for a huge, blow-up media tent provided by the National Guard.

Joe Cahn, studying the sauce piquant preparation like it would be it would have its own section on the SAT test, soaks in the atmosphere.

"The sad thing is that a lot of people think of tailgating as a bunch of drunk guys in the parking lot, when it's really the social activity of getting together," Cahn explains. "It's a family activity. Beer pong and guzzling everything in the lot, that's a sad portrayal.

"Here, listening to Cajun music, a boucherie over there, sauce piquant over here… it don't get no better."

Before he could get out another word, the Commisioner is interrupted by a panicked yell under the blue sauce piquant tent.

"Rice cooker!"

It seems that Tim's spaghetti plate of cords for all the displays had sucked up the voltage to the rice pot. For a Cajun being separated from his squirrel, this qualifies as an emergency beyond Code Red on the Homeland Security scale.

Let's just call it *Code Rouge*.

Half the men within earshot scramble for help; the other half trace the extension-cord tangle as they fathom a myriad of MacGuyver-style solutions.

By 11 a.m., the steamer finally relinquishes itself back to duty. Fox and the Playboys walk off the stage after a marathon set. There is a distinct feeling of calm before the upcoming Tee Cotton storm.

"Especially today, its better pacing than it has been in the past," Jacob Fontenot observes in relief. "We've done a lot of the prep work. We got the Jumbotron (aka the Tee-Tron) already done. We've had a lot of support this year, like with the flags. The Girl Scouts helped set up all the flags last night. The field was all done by the coaches and players from Ville Platte High. I know like as a community project, they've been painting the stadium, steps and all for this game. The bleachers and all are freshly painted by volunteers, some members of the Ville Platte High booster club."

Next up on his dad's checklist is to welcome the KLFY-10 crew (a CBS affiliate out of nearby Lafayette). After dispensing pleasantries with the news team, Fontenot's focus will fall squarely on the afternoon's pep rally frenzy.

A huge tradition of the TCB is Tim and Jacob's self-imposed challenge to hit both schools' pep rallies within a one-hour window, pumping up both gymnasiums with a glance of the trophy, some skits, and anything else to get the rivalry blood pumping. Today will be no different, as they plan to tease Ville Platte High this afternoon from 2:00-2:30 before zooming cross-town via police escort to do it all again at Sacred Heart.

The centerpiece of the cross-town tour – the Tee Cotton trophy – is a definite highlight. The cup is large enough to swallow the state championship trophy other Louisiana schools drool over.

With the pep rally sprint about two hours away, Jacob busies himself with the menial task of removing the UPC tags from the dozens of miniature American flags which were placed by the scouts earlier and now pepper the outer edges of both end zones.

At 12:30 p.m., the activity on the field has turned up a few notches. Katie Johnson of KLFY arrives on the scene. A Florida native, the young blonde reporter seems not quite sure of what to make of the festivities nor the contents of the pot under the blue tent. She chats jovially with the group of men searching for swimming squirrel heads before she makes a beeline for a sandwich waiting for her in the news van. During the same break, Eric Boudreaux – the cameraman that is with her – embraces an offered bowl of sauce piquant like a moppet clasping a Wonka ticket.

While the television crew is taking a short rest, Jennifer Vidrine is combing all corners of the stadium, looking for volunteers to be interviewed by Ms. Johnson. She swipes a few VPH football players that are helping to prepare the field. Jennifer calls parents for permission to get their children on camera. Proud mommas oblige eagerly.

At 1:45 p.m., the red National Guard-sponsored media tent arises like an inflatable tarantula. The spider-like shelter is oddly reminiscent of the structure that housed the rock band U2 on their *360* tour, albeit a micro-sized version. This time, however, instead of providing shelter for four Irish gentlemen pushing the volume limits on their amps, this formation will soon be the home of volunteers and press members pushing the limits of leather belts and elastic waistbands. Roadies with speaker towers are replaced with parent helpers carrying gallons of chicken and sausage gumbo.

One man missing the structure's rise is Dr. Tim. He is busy making a quick Wal-Mart run before returning a bit later to go over his 'to-do' list with Jacob.

When he finally makes it back to base, father and son review the more mundane details of things like extension cords and batteries. They study the list like the Rebel Alliance combing Death Star blueprints. It's not that the plans themselves are that complicated; it's just that the two are about to embark on their pep rally challenge and will not return until well after 3 p.m. There is no room for error at this point.

Tim's voice is now weary and tired; he sounds like a man in desperate need of his second wind.

Twenty minutes later, Dr. Tim and Jacob are crowded together with a police officer in a corner of the Ville Platte High gymnasium. They discuss the logistics as to how best get the Tee Cotton founder and his trophy from one school to the other in a matter of moments.

"From now on, it's going to be '*Boom! Boom! Boom!*'" Jacob explains. "That's one of the coolest things.

"We get the very first part of this pep rally and the very last part of Sacred Heart's pep rally. It's pretty intense to hit two pep rallies in less than a 30-minute span."

It is now 2:23 p.m., and the Bulldogs are running way late with their celebration; students finally begin to file in. The Jerome Vidrine Memorial Trophy sits tantalizingly in center court. It's a fitting setting for a trophy named after one of the Bulldogs' own.[11]

The trophy will sit solitary for a few moments more. After a few final seconds of suspension, cheerleaders spill out to the court. The Ville Platte High football team, defending Tee Cotton champions, runs straight to the cup sitting in the middle of the gym. The athletes make an impromptu Bulldog dogpile as they excitedly jump over each other for a chance to touch the silver bowl. Tubas pump a steady beat as the energy rises in the building.

---

[11] The trophy's namesake was a VPH graduate of the 1960's era. In his life, Vidrine was stricken with Muscular Dystrophy. Neither the ailment nor the accompanying wheelchair could stop him from attending VPH and SHS games, or from raising thousands of dollars for the cause before his life ended from the disease. Dr. Tim is a sucker for that kind of spirit, and named the cup after Jerome in honor of the former Bulldog's fortitude.

If Dr. Tim was in need of a second wind, this was like a tornado.

The floor clears as the PA system shoots out the opening horns of Ying Yang Twins' "Halftime (Stand Up & Get Crunk)." Tim swaggers to the middle. Teasingly, he pops on a pair of sunglasses to the crowd's approval. He displays dance moves not usually seen in the repertoire of a 50-something year old Caucasian male. He acts as his own second line parade as he traces the basketball court boundaries, pointing at groups of kids with both hands in perfect rhythm to the song.

This normally quiet Catholic man may have channeled his inner evangelist last night at the banquet, but today he is calling on the ringmaster inside him. He lifts his hands to ask the students to make some noise for him; they follow his commands all-too happily.

This is Tim's element. This is his Christmas.

He moves back towards center court, where Ville Platte High football coach Roy Serie serves up a dance challenge. The two men throw down to the delight of all in attendance. Coach Serie pulls out the 'Stanky Leg', forcing Dr. Tim to prove that there's more moves in his toolbox than just the 'White Man's Overbite.'

Jacob is running around the gym, taping the dance, perhaps secretly hoping for a YouTube moment or two.

The song ends with the coach and the founder victoriously lifting each other's hands. Tim swipes the trophy and escapes to a waiting police car.

As he vanishes, several unfamiliar, menacing men dressed in black jump onto the gym floor. The crowd is taken aback. After their seemingly uninvited strut to half court, however, the strangers' following actions become all-too familiar. By the time the spectators recognize the guitar riffs of Michael Jackson's 'Beat It' coming thru the P.A., these men are already deep into their routine of re-enacting the dance from the legendary music video.

In the middle of the song, another figure appears. With a singular sequined glove, bouncing Jheri curls and sparkling socks, a Michael Jackson impersonator joins them. The figure pulls out stomps, kicks, and a two-toed balancing act as if this were just another night in Motown in the 1980's.

The man behind the shades is Lee Green, a former Ville Platte High graduate now living in Houston, Texas and making his living as a police officer. A Tee Cotton Bowl enthusiast, he contacted Dr. Tim earlier in the year offering to help out anyway possible. After Dr. Tim talked him out of his first choice – jumping with the skydiving team during the

TCB pregame – he decided to recreate his role as an amazing King of Pop facsimile. It is a job that he and his backup dancers do impressionably well on.

At 2:37 p.m., 'Michael' finishes up. Jacob secures his camera and darts off to his car. Unlike his father, who vanished a few heartbeats earlier, Jacob does not have the privilege of sirens in front of him. The son just hopes there will be no police lights joining up behind him. It's all back roads and prayers if he wants to make the tail end of the Sacred Heart pep rally.

Six minutes later, Tim's son pulls into the Trojans' parking area. Jacob is still unable to go inside the gym as he has to succumb to lookout duties. Somewhere along the way, the cars carrying *Immi Jimmi* MJ and his dance crew fell behind the Tee Cotton's afternoon convoy.

Inside SHS, Jacob's father is giving a speech to the Trojan Nation. It is the same talk he'd given the Bulldogs moments earlier.

Finally, Lee's backup dancers arrive. They wait behind the gym on a sidewalk that splits that building with the school's cafeteria and a small graveyard. Meanwhile, Tim reproduces the Crunk strut he'd pulled off earlier at VPH. Unlike at the Bulldogs' house, there are no Trojan challengers to take on the dancing doctor.

As the music ends, Sacred Heart has a Spinal Tap moment when Tim gets the crowd hyped with cheers of 'MJ! MJ! MJ!'

Only problem is that MJ is still MIA.

To make matters worse, a fog machine pumping out smoke from the locker room sets off the fire alarm in the area. The alarm begins to alternate between distorted screeches and garbled verbal warnings. The spoken alerts sound as if they were recorded by a Star Wars stormtrooper with a hangover and a tracheotomy wand.

The Gloved One finally appears in the middle of the madness, making up for his tardiness with a James Brown split that launches him into 'Thriller,' complete with transformation into werewolf. Whereas no SHS coach dared challenge Tim's prancing to Ying Yang Twins, a bold Sacred Heart football player, Caine Thevenot, decided to sign himself up to Michael's posse. He keeps up rather well.

After the show, Tim heads back to his office. He changes from the split Tee Cotton tee into a nicer, embroidered polo shirt with the game's logo. He comes out of his office with armloads of what looks like a bear costume.

He tosses the outfit next to a Sacred Heart goal pad. In Tee Cotton, each team has its own goal decorated with such to keep the theme of neutrality.

"It's just like the Super Bowl," Tim mentions.

Driving back towards the stadium, it is now 3:30 p.m. A car passes Tim. The car's front doors prop up two banners – on one side is a flag for Tee Cotton, on the other is one for Southern University.

Tim drives slowly through the neighborhood. The Tee Cotton's mastermind has been absent from the field for almost two hours. As he approaches the gates, he scans the area hoping things are falling into place like Tetris pieces. Any less and it could spell disaster.

The radio and television interviews are behind him. Last night, he preached fire and brimstone. This morning, he was up three hours before the sun to oversee a boucherie and show southern hospitality to a football celebrity. This afternoon, he danced like a one-man wrecking crew. The good doctor's been awake for thirteen hours already; he has at least another ten to go.

In the next hour or so, the founder will have to handle a fireworks display setup. He'll also have to verify the arrival of the 1965 VPH team honorees, a parachute squad, and Southern University's elite drum corp.

There's also the part about having to convince somebody to get into a bear suit.

Some might say it takes a crazy man to have that vision, much less to have the determination to pull off that vision successfully.

Not really. It just takes a Cajun.

CHAPTER THREE

E.T. Winds Up in a Sauce

When French Canadians were banished by the British to the Louisiana swamps well over two centuries ago, they transformed those swamps into campgrounds and created a sportsman's paradise. When these same Cajun settlers were so impoverished that they had to scour ditches for dinner, they turned crawfish into a $120,000,000 industry for the state of Louisiana. As this innovative people were busy doing mundane Monday laundry, they just washed happily in rhythm until the scrub board transformed from a primitive household tool to an angelic musical instrument.

Even now, while the rest of the modern world still befuddles itself by trying to make clichéd lemonade out of tired lemons, Cajuns are known to mix the elixir, serve it up ice cold with a squeeze of Louisiana strawberries, and dish it up on side of a feast of *cracklins* and *cochon de lait*.

Today, the Acadian people still ooze the fortitude needed to overcome the biggest of obstacles and turn the worst of situations into a celebration. For those that have a hard time believing such ingenuity against adversity exists in today's Big Box, *iAnything* society, three words need to be remembered:

Curtis Everette Johnson.

Johnson resides in Turkey Creek, Louisiana – a town in Evangeline Parish less than 20 miles north of Ville Platte, with a population of less than 400.

Like most every man born and raised here, Johnson hunts and cleans any deer or squirrel unfortunate enough to cross his path.

Unlike no other man raised here, Johnson was born without arms. He keeps up with the rest of the woods and waters crowd by use of his feet.

Even with his handicap, his parents had decided never to treat him as disabled. Under doctor's advice, they were told to let him learn how to do the things he needed to do.

In this rural parish, that includes knowing how to hunt and fish.

"When you live around Turkey Creek, what else is there to do?" he told the local Ville Platte Gazette newspaper in a September 2009 interview.

It's a legitimate question coming from someone living in a town with a population smaller than that of a Wal-Mart parking lot.

According to the article written by the Gazette's Carissa Hebert, Johnson is quite handy with a fishing pole, too, teaching himself how to bait hooks and string lines. Thanks to his brother Jessie – a welder by trade – Johnson handles everything else on an outdoorsman's checklist rather well, including driving around on a modified four-wheeler and hanging out in his customized deer stand.

"A lot of things I do a little different, but I figured we're all a little different," Curtis told the newspaper for the 2009 article.

His resilience only shows the promise that the people of the area have toward keeping the state a sportsman's paradise.

In fact, it is this level of commitment that causes Ville Platte to become a ghost town the first weekend of every October. That weekend is the official start of squirrel season and as close to an official Cajun holiday as the definition will allow.

The event is so popular, even the schools have been known to lock up the gates and hit the lights.

Sacred Heart High, in particular, has the day off to avoid huge waves of absenteeism.

"Whenever you talk about Ville Plattians and the male culture, about 90 percent of them hunt or fish," explains Ms. Dawn Shipp, assistant principal at Sacred Heart. "Anything they eat either flies, or swims, or climbs a tree."

Of course, one does not have to be a guy with a gun to take part in the festivities. Ms. Shipp recalls how years ago, the girls at school soon picked up on the idea and made up their own parallel holiday, albeit one that traded charge cards for camouflage.

"Just so many of the male students were gone (on first day of squirrel season), that only the female students were there. The females finally said, 'The men are going hunting, we're going shopping!'

"There really was nobody at school, so they decided to call it 'Squirrel Day'."

For a time Ville Platte High also partook in the tradition. Unfortunately, in recent years, outside criticism – from places as far away as the late Paul Harvey's infamous nationwide radio microphone – has forced the public school Bulldogs to break with tradition, at least officially.

But just because the holiday no longer exists on the Evangeline Parish Public Schools calendar does not mean that the students of Ville Platte High still can't try to sneak out. The people from the area are a determined bunch.

Besides, any VPH student that chose to skip would just be acting from example. Most men in the town, regardless of age, grab their shotguns and play hooky on Squirrel Day. Many businesses shutter early. At city hall, Casual Friday has been known to be replaced with Camo Friday in respect for the rodent.

The annual great escape caused Dr. Tim Fontenot to help popularize the phrase 'Cajun Passover' in an interview he did with *Field and Stream* magazine in 2004.

"It's a mass exodus into the woods," he explained to the publication.

As exciting as the opening days of hunting season may be, eventually the hunters have to return home from their mission. If squirrels and shotguns can make Cajun men disappear of the face of the Earth on a Friday and Saturday, then the things not of this world can bring them right back to the ground come Sunday.

Father Gene Tremie of Sacred Heart Catholic Church proudly notes that attendance does not suffer during this time of year.

"They come in late, but they take their obligation seriously," he recalls. "It's been drilled into them. The hunters will come in to be sure they make their Mass."

The priest himself doesn't do much partaking of the activity, confessing he's not the best with a gun. He laughingly admits, "I used to go hunting, and the squirrels were very grateful when I'd go!"

In Cajun country, squirrels are food, and food and religion go hand and hand. Even portion size and spices have denominational ties, according to Joe Cahn, a Louisiana native and chef before he became the Commish.

"Down here, food is a celebration," he states, making an obvious point. "As you go up further, the food is substance. It's not going to be as spicy. But people down here eat for entertainment. This is part of our social life. We perceive food a different way.

"South Louisiana is predominantly Catholic; North Louisiana is predominantly Baptist," he mentions as he explains why portion sizes are so much larger in this area than 45 minutes up Interstate 49. "When we talk about Catholic, we talk about how we can be forgiven by confession; in other forms, abstinence is the way to forgiveness."

Cahn's gastro-theology in a nutshell? A Protestant, raised in modesty, might be offered a pile of food. He may refuse, stating, "No way I can eat all that." A Catholic, offered the same bounty, may exclaim excitedly, "No way! I can eat all that!"

The Commish notes the hearty overtones of Cajun cuisine when compared to the rest of the country. He harkens back to the time he was offered sushi.

"That's sushi?" he remembers telling the server. "In Louisiana, we call that bait! We cut out the middle man."

With food such a part of the lifestyle in Acadiana, there is always the question of 'Where can I get more?' And while Ms. Shipp's assessment of "anything they eat either flies, or swims, or climbs a tree" is quite the case, sometimes it's not enough for a Louisiana sportsman looking for something to snipe, skin, and serve.

Sometimes, a paradise just isn't enough. In this case, a Louisiana boy needs to go interplanetary.

One of the highlights of the 2002 *NFL Films Presents* Tee Cotton Bowl feature, run on ESPN, was a clip of Dr. Tim stirring a huge pot. Smiling, he bragged to the camera, "In Louisiana, we put everything in a sauce. If E.T. landed in South Louisiana, he'd be in a sauce."

It was a cute story for the 95% of the viewing nation not from the Acadiana area. For the five percent from Cajun country, it was a call to the Internet to find when muzzle-load and bow seasons started on Extra Terrestrials. Some hunter probably was dreaming up an alibi during the feature, just in case he had to plead to the warden why he was over his bag limit.

Unfortunately for hunters in the area, sometimes a bit of reality sets in. Perhaps the camo is not washed or the UFO's are scarce. At this point, a trip to the local store has to happen. When it does, many go to Paul's Meat Market and Grocery.

When the customers go, they go any way they can.

"There's a fellow who lives not far down the road who'll ride his horse (to the store) on a regular basis," tells store owner Paul Fontenot. "He'll just ride up to the store, buy something and take off. They'll be people driving their tractors on the road on the way to the fields. A guy cutting his lawn mower will cross the road, get gas, buy a few things, and then take off.

"As long as they come in," the owner grins as he shakes his head.

The variety of food in the area requires strong spices and stronger stomachs. The sheer availability of guilty gastronomic pleasures has created a town full of amateur critics.

"People some other places are like, 'They have the best wine, the best cheese...'" Dr. Tim explains. "Over here (in Ville Platte), my patients have discussed who makes the best cracklins, the best boudin, the best hogshead cheese. They all talk like gourmets... 'He makes the best hogshead cheese, but his cracklins aren't that good....'"

While food, along with the procurement and the heated critique of, is an innate part of life in Ville Platte. Cajuns do not survive by bread alone. They need their radio, too. Homegrown KVPI fits the void nicely, and the station's programming only reflects further how incredibly unique the town is.

The pulse of the station is the *La Tasse de Cafe* Friday morning radio show. Broadcasting bilingually in French and English, the show is not afraid to tackle any controversial subject imperative to Ville Platte's residents. Besides the Tee Cotton Bowl, other important matters that have been debated intensely over the airwaves are: Who grows the best tomatoes in town, which six-man football squad from the 40's reigned supreme, and the proper way to say 'Raccoon' in French.

The small station, housed incognito in a brick building tucked in one of Ville Platte's few neighborhoods, is considered keeper of the Swamp Pop flame. The reputation probably came from the fact that Floyd Soileau once spun the vinyl there in the late 1950's. The DJ went on to found the legendary Floyd's Record Shop and Jin Records, the one-two punch responsible the craze's launch in the 50's.

While 'Swamp Pop' was definitely an idea born and raised in Ville Platte, it took a British journalist to coin the term. Even though the words might not hold the same name recognition as 'Zydeco' or 'Cajun', the tunes may actually enjoy a farther, more mainstream reach than either of its cousins. Music fans might not be able to pinpoint the name of the genre, but the sound is unmistakable ear candy for those whose teenage years revolved around poodle skirts and pompadours.

In essence, there is one way to describe this style of 50's rock and roll. The Swamp Pop sound is a simple gumbo of heartfelt lyrics and unrequited longing framed up against slow swing beats, cry-like-a-baby horn sections and melodic piano runs. Having been painted as 'Fais-do-do meets Fats Domino', the Fat Man from New Orleans borrowed from the genre liberally in his heyday. The Beatles even purloined the style for 'Oh Darling,' a track off of *Abbey Road*.

Homegrown hits that have gone coast-to-coast include 'Just a Dream' by Jimmy Clanton, 'Sea of Love' by Phil Phillips, and the legendary 'Mathilda' by Cookie and the Cupcakes.

Although the town radio station is deeply rooted in traditions such as Swamp Pop, KVPI deserves credit for being progressive enough to try one of the most talked-about stunts in Louisiana prep sports journalism – covering the Tee Cotton Bowl.

No, not the one that had been played for the past decade-plus on the gridiron. High school football games are broadcast every weekend in the fall in every city in the United States.

The Tee Cotton Bowl coverage that KVPI may be most famous for might be the Tee Cotton Bowl that had been played not on any field, but over and over inside Dr. Tim's mind.

There's a reason why some town locals have nicknamed him 'Fried Tim'. Some people have voices in their head; Fontenot had an entire football game.

In 2002, Tim Fontenot grabbed a notepad, a friend, and a blank wall. Together, Dr. Tim and KVPI sports personality Randy Guillory outlined the *Tee Cotton Dream*

Bowl, a game that had been swimming around in the Tee Cotton founder's stadium in his cranium.

What Dr. Tim envisioned was a fantasy match of all-stars from both high schools' histories. He had created rosters that stretched from the new millennium all the way back to the era of six-man teams a half-century ago. Grandfathers faced grandchildren. Athletes with ties to both schools were cloned as needed to fill shoulder pads.

And for one afternoon, all of Ville Platte's hometown heroes – the ones that live on in trophy cases, newspaper clippings and back porch bragging – suited up. They faced each other on an empty wall while two grown men with microphones described what they saw there.

No, the scene wasn't sane.

Inspiration for the Tee Cotton Dream Bowl came from an NFL project where the league took computer stats and matched the greatest professionals of all time.

"I was like, 'that would be cool, but we could do that and make it even better," explained Tim. "We're not constrained; (plus) we can do this on radio. Radio, we can do anything."

Soon after the light bulb went off, Tim buzzed his friend, who at the time was a part-time play-by-play announcer running a t-shirt shop in nearby Pine Prairie.

"I call up Randy," the Dream Bowl dreamer recalls. "We went in his shop, looking at a blank wall. We did a coin toss, then we sat and we scripted the game."

"You see what I have to put up with," laughs now-KVPI sports director Randy Guillory when reminiscing with his friend about the Tee Cotton Dream Bowl.

The sports announcer likes to play innocent when describing the frequent shenanigans the duo gets into. Often, Guillory will turn to a red-faced, 'Who? Me?' grin in his defense. However, the halo should be taken with a pinch of *Chachere's*.[12] The KVPI announcer can be slick when needed, and knows just when to crank up the boyish charm. In fact, the more rascal side of Guillory is known to pull such stunts as announcing during real football broadcasts when he's hungry for gumbo, just to see if anyone listening will light up his personal cell phone with a post-game invite.

Together, rascal Randy and touched Tim plotted out the details of a game that required a bit of time travel, a dash of duplication, and sometimes both.

Certain athletes, such as Ville Platte High's Roy Serie, who in reality played as a Bulldog and now coaches them, appeared in both roles in the fan-fiction version.

---

[12] **Chachere's** (*sha-shir-REES*), as in *Tony Chachere's Creole Seasoning*, a popular local seasoning used like salt.

Just like the real Tee Cotton, the good doctor tried his best not to play favorites. Keeping neutral, Tim wouldn't even allow one make-believe team hold the home field advantage for too long.

"The game was so big, we couldn't play it at one stadium, so (at halftime) we moved it," Fontenot recalls.

True to Tee Cotton traditions, he also tried his best to keep the pageantry of real football in his fake game.

The neutrality effort was a success in the script. The fictional opening ceremonies, well, not so much. At least not after the live invocation that was a part of it all.

"We released doves, like they did in Super Bowl I," Tim laughs. "But people started shooting, so we had to stop it. They were shouting 'There's sauce tonight!'"

Even the sponsors were fictional. Other than advertisements for Fontenot Physical Therapy, every commercial was a product of the mind from Tim and Randy. Each spot plugged a business that no longer exists in the town.

"Some people listened to the game just to hear from the old sponsors," Tim remembers.

The men re-enacted the commercials of days gone by, including spots for movies like 'King Kong Versus

Godzilla' at one of the two long-since closed theaters in town.

At the end of Tim's dream, Sacred Heart won 36-33 on a deflected pass, caught by a lineman and returned for a score.

"He (Steven David, a Sacred Heart lineman) was trying to score, and he ran into the Stanford band," the dreamer remembers. "People had rushed the field, and he ran into the tuba player."

Yes, the Stanford band was there somewhere inside the founder's head, too.

It must've been a sight to see Tim and Randy record the event, giving play-by-play on the greatest game to ever be played on an empty brick-and-mortar canvas.

There they were, two grown men staring into nothingness shouting phrases like "He stiff-armed the drummer! Oh the humanity!" into headphones.

"We'd jump and holler and scream at the blank wall," Tim remembers. "We incorporated the Immaculate Reception, the Tuck Rule, all these great plays."

Once the game was recorded, Randy – the more technically savvy, if not the (arguably) more stable of the two – took the tapes and mixed in sound effects and crowd cheers from McNeese State college football games.

"It sounded like, believe it or not, like a real game," Guillory remembers proudly. "We didn't hold anything back. I took the game with me and broke it down, and added the individual sound effects on it. It was a production."

Once recorded, all that was left was the airing. The Dream Bowl was supposed to be a highlight of Tee Cotton III week, the ultimate hype machine for the event. Unfortunately, it's hard to run a hype machine if the town is running off of generators.

While the Tee Cotton Bowl usually brings in spectators from all over, TCB III played host to the most unwanted and uninvited of visitors: Hurricane Lili.

The fourth hurricane of the Atlantic season that year, Lili seemed determined to make a beeline for Cajun country. She lashed out at Louisiana with wind gusts of 120 miles per hour. The storm left almost $800 million in damage to the Bayou State and over a quarter-million without power.

Many of those residents came from Acadiana. At that point, Tim and Randy's Dream Bowl had to be sidelined for a nightmarish reality.

"We were barely on the air, running on generators. It was a mess," Randy remembers.

Tim adds, "We were almost under Marshall Law. (KVPI) was like 'We have free ice over here; we have supplies over there.'"

But Cajuns do not give up easily. Even though the Dream Bowl did not air when scheduled, it did air... over... and over... and over again.

"Randy said, 'We got this thing sitting over here,'" Tim explains. "LSU was playing in a bowl that year (actually, the *actual* Cotton Bowl). So we ran it before LSU's New Year's game. It was so popular that we played it again one Sunday before the NFL playoffs."

While whipping out his boyish 'Who, me?' grin once more, Randy makes a final note.

"Let me make something perfectly clear. This man (Dr. Tim) came up with all of that. I'm just an accessory to the crime – a proud accessory, but an accessory.

"We think alike, unfortunately."

But it's exactly moments and friendships like this that makes life in Acadiana exactly what it is.

If Cajun heritage can be broken into four basic elements, those elements would be: food, music, perseverance, and a dash of crazy. The essence found in those four items causes every day lived in the Acadiana triangle to have the potential to be a celebration. These same ingredients keep the Tee Cotton Bowl running, Swamp Pop pumping, and squirrels scared stiff in the town of Ville Platte.

While food, music, and a dash of crazy make life in Cajun country a joy instead of a mere existence, none of those three ingredients could exist without the fourth element of perseverance.

It is that perseverance that has allowed the Cajun people to grow a strong backbone in the face of persecution. From their Nova Scotia flight centuries ago to the problems out of today's headlines, the people of Ville Platte walk tall and daring in the face of adversity.

Amazingly, threats to the their way of life still come today, from people who refuse to wrap their heads around the *joi de vivre* inherent in crawfish boils and Cajun waltzes.

Adversities that challenge Ville Platte, its schools, and its bowl game are out there. Perplexingly, the some of the most devastating bullying ever to face the town had come from a courthouse just down the road.

CHAPTER FOUR

The Game That Should Not Exist

If Ville Platte sits on top of the Acadiana triangle, the town also sits inside the epicenter of long-simmering coals of racial tension.

Eighty miles due north of the town uneasily rests the city of Jena, site of the famous 'Jena 6' trials of 2007. It was there that a march was held to protest criminal charges brought upon six African-American students who assaulted a fellow Caucasian classmate at Jena High School. Nationwide media attention bombarded the area for weeks on end, and the small town of 3,000 had swollen to five times its size through the mostly unwelcomed aid of journalists, protesters, and curious onlookers.

Closer to Ville Platte, tension may be less intense and run lower on the nation's radar, but it still does surely run. Columnists and bloggers might not give the same ink or bandwith to Acadiana that they gave to Jena, but the lack of coverage certainly does not equate to the lack of issues.

Ville Platte is a relative calm eye in a hurricane of injustice. The city is a hub of reason sitting in a wheel of still-smoldering prejudices.

Head 20 miles southeast of Ville Platte and one will find segregated baseball fields, as many parents in the small town of Washington choose to sign up their children for the all-white, private 'Independent' program rather than enroll their kids in the public recreational league.

Every now and then, come springtime, another school in the Acadiana area will make headlines for issues regarding desegregating proms or canceling formals due to one underlying racial issue or another.

No town in the United States – north or south – can ever admit to be 100% in racial harmony without some skepticism at the claim. It is safe to say, however, with a degree of certainty, that the townspeople of Ville Platte have become a shining light in Louisiana. The town presents an example to be modeled and admired.

While the local citizenry's ability to get along is highly regarded, this characteristic has produced an odd side effect. The town that makes a deliberate point to not exclude anyone occasionally becomes the victim of their surrounding communities' indifference.

Perhaps it's time the rest of Cajun country give them credit.

"Ville Platte has always had a prejudice against it," Dr Tim recalls. "I don't know why. White and black people (from out the area) are like 'Ville Platte? *Meh*'."

The white Tee Cotton Bowl founder gives his own spin on why Ville Platte has avoided the problems of its neighbors.

"The best thing about Ville Platte is that there is no class distinction. The people that are really powerful out here like the sheriff, doctors... they're powerful because they recognize everybody. They recognize the poor guy on the street. They shake his hand. We need each other. And the fact is if you want to be upper class in Ville Platte, you're going to be upper class by yourself.

"The big phrase is, 'He's got a lot of money, but he's not very nice.' And that's what people will say, white and black. It doesn't matter who you are. (Around here) nobody's better than you, but you're not better than anybody.

"It forces us to get along, to coexist. We need each other. It makes it special over here. Over here, people won't mess with you. It's almost reverse discrimination. You think you're too good? We won't mess with you."

Fontenot continues, as he is prone to do, unable to tell as story without giving some sort of sports reference.

"Like at the ball parks (in Ville Platte), the kids play all-star together," Dr. Tim offers. "There's a kid right now; a doctor's son, a child of privilege. And you've got a black kid; a black kid right now, whose mom and dad works, but a different kind of culture. Then you've got a poor white kid whose momma isn't married, has two or three kids, daddy was on drugs, but they're all playing ball together. They all like each other. The kids take care of each other. Everybody brings something to the table. It's great. It's awesome to have a place like this. It's wonderful to live over here because you need everybody."

Dr. Tim's thoughts are echoed throughout the community, both black and white.

Jennifer Vidrine, when not busying herself with the task of being the boisterous, self-proclaimed number one Bulldog fan, is the assistant executive director for the Evangeline Community Action Agency. After graduating Ville Platte High in 1976 and going on to LSU to study

Psychology, she went back home to help. Today, she sees things from ground zero, as her job requires her to bring aid to Evangeline Parish's most needy citizens, including the elderly and low-income residents.

"We don't care what color you are," Ms. Vidrine, an African-American, says excitedly and unprompted about her hometown. "We don't care what socio-economic background you are from. We don't care if you come from a single-parent or a two-parent household. We don't get caught up in all those superficial things. It's nothing but community in Ville Platte. We have compassion; we care about each other."

Another African-American and Bulldog alum to agree with Fontenot's observations is Chief of Police Neal Lartigue. A graduate of Ville Platte High in 1984, his job is made easier every time racial situations skip over his hometown.

"The reason we avoid (tension) is the town is close," Lartigue says. "The people are close. We have a town of 8,500 people and basically everybody knows everybody. Either you worked together or played ball against each other, because these schools were here and people came up together. Now they're the adults. I think that's what keeps the riots out.

"Insofar as the riots in (other area schools), we have two great high schools here in town. The teachers here –

most of them are from here, grew up here, played ball here. The principals that are here grew up here and went to school here (at VPH) or Sacred Heart. They know the kids' parents. It helps keep things kind of down and quiet."

This is not to imply that there haven't been growing pains in the town; it's just that the town has taken the pains and tried to heal the wounds, rather than open up and re-salt them again and again.

As Sacred Heart Booster Club president Mark Buller will attest, to heal wounds correctly sometimes you need the Doctor. A graduate of the school in 1980, he remembers what the city championship was like back before Fontenot came forth with his Tee Cotton brainstorm in 1999.

"Back then, it was a bitter rivalry," recalls Buller of his time at SHS in the late 1970's. "They (Ville Platte High) didn't trust us, we didn't trust them. It was a bitter cross-town rivalry. The parents didn't trust leaving their kids alone. Actually, one time we had to get the sheriff's posse because of people breaking into cars.

"My freshman or sophomore year, we played them on a Sunday afternoon. It was more the fans (causing problems). The players, I don't think, were that mad at each other. But the fans were typical black/white, into the racial thing."

Fast forward two decades and the SHS alumnus would hear Dr. Tim's idea. Like many of the townsfolk who grew up during rougher times, the booster club member considered Fontenot to be a bit touched, and not by an angel.

"I thought he was out of his mind," Buller recalls. "I was like, 'Tim, this is not going to work. You're going to spend a lot of money, a lot of time. You're going to get frustrated.'

"But he kept plugging. After about the second year or third year, it was like this is the best thing that's ever happened to our community. It was like divine intervention or something that made this happen. It changed the attitude of the fans, young and old, the parents, the teachers, (and) the business people. They just brought the camaraderie."

One of the amazing byproducts of the past ten years of the Tee Cotton era is that the rival teams are not only not archenemies anymore, but they are actually fervent supporters of each other's endeavors.

The Sacred Heart head booster revels in the way the teams now look out for each other.

"Ville Platte High usually has a very good track team, a good basketball team," Buller compliments. "Our kids support them. I remember the past for the past four or five years, in the Top 28 (state tournament) they (VPH) got to pass on Main Street. We'd take our high school kids at eight o'clock in the morning; line them up on Main Street with purple and white signs.

"They did the same thing for us last year when we went to the football playoffs. They're cheering us on. The last couple of years, when we went to the playoffs, we had bonfires here for our kids. We invited Ville Platte High to come over. Their cheerleaders came, cheered with our cheerleaders to fire everybody up the night before the playoff games."

Moments like these helped transform Dr. Tim's status in the community from eccentric to visionary.

"Seven or eight years ago, I'd never dreamed it would've happened," the booster president admits. "Without Tim, it never would've happened. I can actually say, from my own experience – because I have a daughter in cheerleading, I have a son that played for four years – I can honestly say that their attitude towards race is a lot better than my attitude was growing up. I guess it's the way we were brought up. Their attitude is much more positive and forgiving and accepting. I credit all that to it to Tim."

"The Tee Cotton Bowl bridges all kinds of gaps – social, racial, church groups, economic, cultural," Dr. Tim proudly analyzes. "It just bridges gaps when God touches it. At the game, you feel God's joy. People just smile.

Like any proud dad, the father of the TCB beams when he shares stories of how the teams have gone out their way to support each other.

"(TCB) has definitely improved relations. It doesn't stop at the game. It goes on year round. This past year (the week after the 2008 TCB), Sacred Heart played Opelousas Catholic on a Thursday night. Ville Platte High's fans were so appreciative. The principal asked 'How can we repay you? What can we do for Sacred Heart?'

"I said the best thing you can do for them is cheer for them.

"So they brought the whole team to Opelousas, brought them in their jerseys. The Ville Platte High kids all sat on Sacred Heart's side. The people from Opelousas were like, who are all these kids?

"The Ville Platte High kids started playing the drums from (Sacred Heart's) drum line. Sacred Heart players were like 'Wow, they're pulling for us'. Sacred Heart came from behind and won.

"They (SHS) didn't talk about their fans; they talked about how Ville Platte High came cheer for them. The Ville

Platte High kids even went on the field after the game and prayed with them."

Ville Platte High athlete Jesse James West, Jr. summed up the feelings of his team when he said, "I wish we (Ville Platte High and Sacred Heart) could combine and just make a big 6-A school."

With all of the bridge-building going on under the watchful eye of Dr. Tim, it is unfortunate that someone would bring a flamethrower to try and burn it all down.

It is more unfortunate that the person would be a federal judge.

Almost a half-century ago, in 1965, a desegregation lawsuit was filed against the Evangeline Parish School Board by Ms. JoAnn Graham, under the allegations that the board ran a racially-segregated school system. Several factors were highlighted for improvement, including student assignments, faculty assignments and facilities.

For decades, the case lay dormant in inactivity. While the courts remained silent, wounds began to heal and a town began to mature. But the courts peeled scabs in 2008 when Federal Judge Tucker Melancon of the Western District of Louisiana, who had came into active management of the case around the year 2000, threatened to dissolve

Ville Platte High and send the students to the four corners of Evangeline Parish.

The possibility was so real that the Tee Cotton Bowl victory photo from 2008 had both teams posing around the Vidrine Cup, rather than just the victor. Dr. Tim wanted both teams to be in the photo as a final memory.

Threats to shut down Ville Platte High were coming down from the bench early and often. There was simply no way to even know if the bowl, much less one of its participants, was still going to be in existence by 2009.

If Ville Platte High were to be dissolved, then so would be the Tee Cotton.

Dr. Tim had no interest in having to start a new tradition from scratch by bringing in another team to replace the Bulldogs. The TCB was to honor the city of Ville Platte, and the teams would have to come from inside the city limits. Otherwise, he would have been happy to put an asterisk and an Amen on his project.

More stressed than Tim was the athletic staff of Ville Platte High, who chewed many a fingernail just worrying about their jobs.

Roy Serie, head coach of Ville Platte High, remembers the additional pressure the desegregation plan had put on his role.

"My first year taking over (as head coach in 2007), we didn't know who the coach was going to be," due to the court's faculty assignment oversight, he recalls. "We were in (the courthouse) waiting room going into August and we didn't know who the coach was going to be. I ended up being the coach.

"The second year, we didn't know if we were going to have a school. We're in the waiting room not knowing if we were going to have a school. So we had to deal with that. The decision wasn't made last year until after the Tee Cotton Bowl, so we were playing like it was going to be the last one.

"This year (2009) we know we have a school. It's a good feeling to know that. In fact, we still don't know. We never know. We just play each one like it's going to be the last one."

The judge may see things in black-and-white; the kids of the town do not.

Cole LeCoq can attest. LeCoq, one of a scattered handful of white Ville Platte High football players, spent the first half of his academic life at Sacred Heart before transferring to Ville Platte in seventh grade. He had no problems with the switch.

"Even when I came over here (to VPH), you would think that (race) would matter," the athlete explains. "But over here, it's just not like that. I went to the school across the tracks, and it was never a big deal. I was never the odd guy out because I was the little white kid that used to go to Sacred Heart. It was *never* like that," LeCoq says, making sure to emphasize the adverb.

This is a town that really embraces its public school. Assistant principal of Sacred Heart, Dawn Shipp, who previously worked at Ville Platte High, notes that even federal court orders could not shake parents' faith in VPH. Ms. Shipp references the lack of transfer students to Trojan country as evidence.

"This year (2009), we are seeing a little bit more (influx of students at SHS), but not as much. Because there's such a camaraderie with Ville Platte High, we see more kids come to us from Grand Prairie[13] than we do from Ville Platte."

Unfortunately, through all the racial growth and maturity for the town, somebody forgot to tell the courts that the town and the parish grew up. A desegregation plan that was ordered to be filed in the court in 1965 was never drawn up and submitted. Because of this, the case was allowed to be reopened.

---

[13] Grand Prairie is a neighboring community, just across the border in St. Landry Parish.

The adage *"If it ain't written down, it didn't happen"* could never be more devistatingly true.

While the motive of desegregation seems idealistic and American enough, as if the judge were donning red, white, and blue angel's wings under his robe, many believed the devil was in the docket.

One major criticism of Judge Melancon has been that he concerns himself not with the spirit of desegregation, but with the detailed micromanagement of the school boards that must carry out the orders. He was called out for such by the Fifth Circuit Court of Appeals in New Orleans in an appellate ruling on *NANS*.

In 2003, Evangeline Parish began drafting out a desegregation plan for the courts. An appeal was filed by the local chapter of the *National Association of Neighborhood Schools*. The organization consisted of parents and other community members who were most concerned with school assignment and the possibility of Ville Platte High students being moved and the school closing. NANS argued, among other reasons, that parents had a right to enroll children in the school nearest their home in order to keep the identity of their local community. Although Ville Platte High was over 70% African-American, NANS saw this as a result of geographic location and not of backroom gerrymandering.

Melancon denied the group input and the matter went to the Fifth District Court of Appeals in 2005.

Although Melancon's ruling to silence NANS was upheld by the three-member judges' panel, it did not come without heavy criticism.

The panel said the court's tone and length of its opinions "suggests personal involvement in the case that approaches more of an administrative than a judicial role." The appellate judges admonished Melancon for interfering with the Evangeline Parish School Board, citing he was helping to "create a perception, whether justified or not, that the board had forfeited its role to the district court."[14]

Melancon was recognized at the same hearing to have contacted school board members personally to chastise them on their voting records.

The Fifth District Court of Appeals had ordered Melancon's U.S. District Court to "limit itself to traditional judicial decision-making rather than school administration, and refrain from day-to-day management of its decrees."

Yet, a year and a half after the formal dress-down, Melancon still dabbled in day-to-day involvement of the parish school systems. His particular judicial style included

---

[14] *Graham, et al v. Evangeline Parish School Board v. Evangeline Parish Chapter National Association of Neighborhood Schools, et al,* U.S. Court of Appeals, Fifth Circuit, transcript, p. 13

tossing several contempt charges at the board, sometimes even playing part of accuser and magistrate. At least one board member was jailed.

In addition to accusations of judicial overreach by his peers, Melancon's charm from the bench won him very few friends in the Evangeline neighborhoods.

During a hearing on July 24, 2008, Melancon compared his role in the desegregation case as "kind of like a sanitation worker, the man and lady that picks up the garbage." Later in the hearing, he would say that handling the case "is kind of like picking up the garbage on July 5th."[15]

In the same court transcript, the judge criticized his perceived version of the town by saying, "It doesn't escape me that there is a general deterioration that I've seen in this city," even though he admitted having not visited Ville Platte "often, anymore."[16]

Maybe if he'd come visit the city at least once a year on the day of the Tee Cotton Bowl, Melancon would have chosen his words more carefully. Plus, he could have changed his mind while chomping on a boudin link and

---

[15] *Graham, et al v. School Board of Evangeline Parish*, July 24, 2008, hearing transcript, pg. 6
[16] hearing transcript, July 24, 2008, pg. 16

cracklins. After all, the real world of Ville Platte revolves around gridiron and grub, not gavels and gag orders.

When the people of the parish felt that Judge Melancon tried to force a tax on them, his credibility with the residents took a major hit. The judge made no secret of his desire for the parish to build a new campus outside of city limits, even though the proposed site would be too far out for a clientele used to walking or riding bikes to school.[17] There were threats and promises to shut down Ville Platte High all together and move the students to other high schools in the far reaches of a parish 680 square miles in area.

The townspeople took the alleged bullying-from-the-bench seriously. Here was a magistrate – known by educators as 'the scary judge' and by the local blogosphere as 'Tuck-Head' – which the people of Ville Platte believed to be trying to impose his will no matter what the price tag.

But Evangeline Parish was not the only parish to suffer through the judge's rezoning demands. Evidence of the judge's other rezoning efforts rested in next-door St. Landry Parish, where a riot kicked off the 2009 school year. At North Central in LeBeau, ten students, including four who were 17 or over, were charged in the incident. The event, believed to have been sparked by territorial issues,

---

[17] hearing transcript, July 24, 2008, pg. 18

happened soon after the school board there was forced to relocate students under one of Melancon's orders. The school, a former traditional high school, had been compelled to take in students from fifth grade on up, from a more scattered geographical region.

In the case of *Graham,* the judge – originally appointed by President Bill Clinton – was insisting on holding high ground on a case almost a half-century old, forgetting that most of those who caused the injustices of that era are no longer exchanging oxygen for carbon dioxide.

The people of the town were in no mood to pay taxes to chase ghosts.

Dr. Chuck Aswell, a longtime friend of Fontenot, believes that just the idea of fighting the judge's twisted spins on desegregation united, rather than polarized, the town.

Dr. Aswell ponders, "It's crazy that Fox News and other places (that report on race) don't see it, that it's all about relationships. And now they're trying to take Ville Platte High away from us? But what's wrong? What's wrong with having your own social identity? There's nothing wrong with it.

"What's wrong is having people who don't want to do something, do something that they don't want to do. Most of the people that were fighting for Ville Platte High School were people from Sacred Heart, because they (VPH parents) didn't have enough money or power or anything to fight for their school. They didn't know how to go and what to do. They knew how to voice their opinion, but what else?"

Richard Vidrine, a member of the 1965 undefeated Bulldog squad, explains the fight.

"I think he (the judge) used the wrong tactics. He tried to jam a tax to build a new school. He threatened the people with that, and we voted it down three times. It made it look like people were against education.

"That judge, the way he went about it, he burned too many bridges. He threatened. He thought he was going to hold that against the people and make us vote for a tax. We didn't do it. Now he has to crawfish back.[18] Now the building is strong enough to keep open."

Judge Melancon himself fulfilled Vidrine's prophecy of crustaceanal proportions during a desegregation hearing held on December 22, 2009, after the town rejected the tax to move the school for the third time.

From the bench, the judge had described a recent visit to VPH:

---

[18] *crawfish (v.) – to backtrack from an earlier threat.* Just as a mudbug will flail his claws in a fight, only to crawl backwards when intimidated, a big talker will sometimes instinctively back off from an earlier boast once he can sense an impending defeat. The term is a popular colloquialism in Cajun country.

"We were there the better part of the day," he remembered. "You can keep one class quiet and you can keep another class quiet, because you know the federal judge is coming and the lawyers are coming and the school board members are coming and the superintendent's coming, for a little bit of time, but you cannot – there's no way – and I taught school for two years. Maybe it was too long and maybe not long enough. You can't control the whole school for a day.

"And what I'm talking about is what I saw in those classrooms were not only the kids that were really into what they were doing, but I saw teachers that still had fire in their eyes. And I taught long enough to see the ones that are asleep at the switch and have given up and are getting a check. Maybe they were never good, or maybe they gave up because of the politics, or whatever the reason, but you've got some great teachers that I saw. You had wonderful instruction going on. And the kids, when they broke between classes and went to lunch – I mean, you can't fake those kinds of things. That school has gotten such a bad rap, I think, from some people who are well-intentioned, but they just don't understand."[19]

---

[19] *Graham, et al v. School Board of Evangeline Parish*, December 22, 2009, hearing transcript, pg. 22

While that statement may or may not fit the Cajun definition of the *verb* "crawfish", the words were close enough for the townsfolk to run to the store for the corn and potatoes.

To be fair, the tax issue was not without it's supporters. Jennifer Vidrine was a fervent grass-roots organizer of the movement to build a new facility. She attended the court hearings and debated at school board meetings for the new building. Ms. Vidrine even earned the clout for some face time with Melancon.

She feels that the perception of the judge as a heavy-handed autocrat may have cost the town the new school.

"I think (it hurt) because people have preconceived notions that he was going to dictate to us what he wanted."

Ms. Vidrine goes on to say she would not mind if the issue were revived, this time on terms planned by the school board and the community rather than the courts. In fact, she's anxious to accept the challenge to restart the campaign if this happens.

The lady who headed up the failed fight three times promises, "If I had to do it a fourth time, I would do it all over again."

In defeat, Ms. Vidrine still found a victory of sorts. She points out that even though the issue did divide the town, it did not divide the people.

While the community activist found herself in the difficult position debating and disagreeing with others in the close-knit community, friends included, she is proud that everyone handled themselves like adults.

"(Everyone understood) this is a democracy. They had every right to vote against the tax; we had every right to vote for the tax."

She also goes as far as to compliment the kids of both schools, raised on the tenants of the Tee Cotton, who did not step into an *'Us versus Them'* battle.

"It did not separate Sacred Heart and Ville Platte High students," Vidrine explained proudly. "They still had love for each other. Relationships did not change."

While the community held together even in their disagreement, the judge that once talked about a town's "deterioration" and his role in the case as "picking up garbage" had come away impressed. It makes one wonder what would have happened if he had visited on Tee Cotton Week.

With the court's new outlook comes a new lease on life for the Bulldogs. Should things continue to impress through 2012, the judge has promised to remove his oversight.[20]

It's a good thing, too. With the doors staying open for the future, the town can sit back and relish on those that passed through the VPH threshold in previous years, and continue to put the Bulldog Nation on the map for much more positive reasons.

---

[20] *Graham, et al v. School Board of Evangeline Parish*, Dec 22, 2009, hearing transcript, p. 31

CHAPTER FIVE

Building the Old School

Had the taxes passed and the town of Ville Platte funded a high school outside of the city limits, or had the judge gone through on his threat to spread the children over the 680 square miles of Evangeline Parish, the touchstone for almost a century's worth of small-town memories would have vanished with the buses. While the pre-WWII monolith that is Ville Platte High would have most probably lived on solely as a traditional middle school,[21] the new facade and use for the facility would have stuck out like an Amish butter churner at an Apple Store.

---

[21] Ville Platte High currently operates as a 5-12 school.

Just like an abandoned Pizza Hut that gets transformed into a law office, something would not have been right about the alteration to a school retro-fitted exclusively for the tween set. There would always be a lingering feeling that something else should be there on West Cotton Street.

The change in use would have had one greatly saddening effect – it would have easily accelerated the demise of some wonderful memories and tall tales that exist in a town that thrives on them.

No one passes by that Pizza Hut-turned-law office and says, "You know, I brought your mother to that law office on our first date; I spilled Pepsi on her." Likewise, Bulldog alumni, when witnessing the *Pheneas and Ferb* set scatter the campus rather than the prom and homecoming crowd, would have a harder time retaining ownership of those fondest – and not so fondest – of times.

A new school could have permanently damaged these memories. For a Bulldog alum to pledge old reminiscences to a new facility outside of city limits would be akin to asking a kid in a divorced family to automatically love 'new mom'.

An even worse scenario would have been if the judge's spiteful threats to dissolve the high school altogether came to fruition. If that would have taken place, alumni would not even have had a 'new mom' to cling to.

Orphaned, they would have watched their heritage get tossed to the wind, their hearts hammered by a gavel until every ounce of Bulldog blood had been pounded to plasma.

A shame. One can only imagine the number of spirits and spectres walking through 80-year old hallways and the amount of yellowed newsprint clipped and pressed into scrapbooks that generated from Bulldog Central.

From the six-man teams of the 1940's to the Tee Cotton era of the 2000's, any old man worthy of his morning coffee or any grandmother worthy of her refrigerator magnets have their own memories to share.

There were hometown greats like Greg LaFleur – who played the first 'city-championship'-era game against Sacred Heart in 1975, before swapping his Bulldog helmet for an LSU Tiger one (and then trading that hat for those of the St. Louis Cardinals and Philadelphia Eagles).

There were special squads, like the 1980 VPH football team that produced eight shutouts in the season.

The high school even has had its share of super fans, such as Jerome Vidrine, the alum from the 1960's that didn't let little things like a wheelchair or Muscular Dystrophy keep him from bleeding purple and white on the sidelines every fall.

And then there was the team of infamy – the 1965 undefeated team.

The legendary squad is still bragged on today as townsfolk recall how they destroyed all comers on their way to the 1965 State Champ....

Er, scratch that. The team didn't qualify for the Louisiana state title...but they did go to the Pony Bowl.

Yeah. The Pony Bowl. It can be explained.

For the record, the Bulldogs won that one, too, beating Crowley High (another Acadiana-area school) for the Pony proclamation privilege, 12-0.

The title came with all the prestige you'd expect.

So how does a team like the 1965 VPH squad run the tables and still get overlooked for a chance at the state hardware?

In the 1962, 1963, and 1964 seasons, the Bulldogs put up woefully matching 1-9 records. No one expected the miracle that would occur the next year, not even Coach Max Hamlin, who only scheduled four district games for the 1965 campaign.

Rules at the time required a team to have five district games to be considered for state contention.

"I guess if you backed it up 10-15 years, we had a hard time winning district games, if any games," recalls Leland Vidrine, one of the members of the 1965 team of legend.

"But we went undefeated – we played our district games, and we beat seven teams that did go to the state playoffs!" adds teammate Richard Vidrine with a bit of pride, as if the games were held last week, rather than almost a half-century ago.

The two hometown legends remember their days on the gridiron as days of extreme antics.

One memory that sticks out to them is the time the school was doused in the middle of the day with foreboding messages from the sky.

"In our time, they flew propaganda," Leland recalls. "They'd drop leaflets from airplanes. One time we were playing Menard; they were in the playoffs that year."

The papers contained ominous warnings that VPH had no chance against the opposition.

Richard Vidrine, after 44 years of investigating, finally cracked the case.

"I found out how it happened," he sleuths. "It was Wilbert Ardoin and Vic Dupuy (two fellow VPH classmates). They did it to fire us up. They pretended to be people from

Menard High, tossing leaflets from a crop duster explaining how the Eagles were going to beat the Bulldogs."

It wasn't a Twitter tweet, but it definitely did get the point across back in the day.

When speaking of hometown heroes, even legends have *their* legend, and for the 1965 team that role is neatly filled by Glenn LaFleur.

Donnie Perron, Glenn's teammate during the 1965 run, recalls the time that not even a concussion could penetrate his teammate's hard head.

"Glenn had gotten hurt about mid-season, he'd gotten into a wreck and had a concussion," recalls Perron. "He was still in the hospital when we were playing Eunice (High School). He checked out the hospital while we were playing the game – the doctor didn't even check him out, he just left. He went to the stadium, got dressed out, and just ran on the field and played.[22]

"It was uplifting to see him come," Perron admits. "It was a big game. Very seldom did we beat Eunice, and it was homecoming.

---

[22] At risk of re-animating an already dead catchphrase, it must be said: *Kids, please don't try this at home.*

"A lot of parents were betting – our parents were betting against their parents; when they saw Glenn, a lot of their parents began rescinding their bets."

LaFleur's intensity carried on into his college years. His jersey, 40, would be the first ever retired from the University of Southwest Louisiana, now known as University of Louisiana– Lafayette. He also earned a trip to Denver when drafted by the AFL-era Broncos.

In the 1980's, LaFleur passed his hard-nosed football philosophy onto a new generation when he took over as chief whistle-blower at Ville Platte High. His coaching strategies were 'character-building', to put the situation in gentlemen's terms.

"Did I tell you about the time we came back from a game, and we lost, and I pulled the bus up into the garage and I said, 'Don't get undressed. We're going to stay and practice another two hours.'?" Glenn says, grinning in his recollection.

The old coach refers to another time that his players were so steeped into his philosophy that he needed not speak a word to them to get his message across.

"One time we had a scrimmage; Crowley kicked our butt. We had a good team that went 9-1. After the scrimmage, Crowley left. I looked at my team and asked,

'Are you satisfied?' and they said 'No'. I asked, 'Did you play well?' and they said 'No'.

"I said, 'Then you know what to do.'"

The athletes began running 100-yard sprints all by themselves, without another word of instruction from their leader.

"They ran until they had enough. I didn't make them do it. They just knew."

One player of the era who drank Coach Lafleur's Kool-Aid, literally, was Tracey 'Big-T' Jagneaux.

"I'll never forget," the class of '85 graduate remembers, "We had this thing my junior year. Hardly anybody played both ways. We were just fortunate enough to have enough people to go offense and defense. So we had the first offensive unit and the first defensive unit. The cheerleaders made some Kool-Aid.

"Coach said, 'whoever wins the battle goes and gets the Kool-Aid.'"

"Man, We battled for that Kool-Aid. The offense wins the series and he tells us, 'Ya'll go get some Kool-Aid.'

"So we go run, and we drink as much as we can. Then he goes, 'Ya'll finished? Ya'll go get some more Kool-Aid.'

"Stupid us, we go back and get more grape Kool-Aid. We start scrimmaging again. Guess what? We're cramping up. We're throwing up all over the place."

Lesson learned. Apparently learned well, too. Jagneaux eventually became a coach himself. He has stayed at home in Ville Platte, and has bounced back-and-forth for years in assistant coaching roles at both Sacred Heart and Ville Platte High.

The Kool-Aid that Jagneaux consumed had a bit of magic in the mix. For at least the first ten years of Tee Cotton, whichever side he was coaching for was the team that also brought home the Vidrine Cup. This streak has given him the reputation of being the Tee Cotton Bowl's unofficial good-luck charm.

Big-T looks at his time under LaFleur's somewhat unorthodox, discipline-oriented style as a privilege.

"It was fun, because we respected the coach. When I looked at Coach Glenn, I didn't fear him; I respected him. Whenever he said to go out and do something, you did it, because it was just inside of you to go do it. He instilled that inside of you. He was hardcore, but you just did things that way. That's why we were so successful. We won several district championships. We were in the playoffs almost every year, just because it was hardcore, and it's just what you did."

Some athletes like Jagneaux walk proud when they survive a coach. Others walk proud when they survive, period.

Such is the case of Jesse James West, Sr., a Bulldog that would graduate in 1988, three years after Jagneaux.

West Sr. had a solid high school career, including a brag-worthy 22-tackle night under homecoming lights one season. He had a promising future at the next level, with an athletic scholarship to Texas A & M.

He also had a job working with his dad at a lumber yard.

Heading to work one night, a deer jumped into his windshield, wrecking the vehicle. The scholarship was gone in a split-second.

College football teams have no need for quadriplegics.

"I was paralyzed from the neck down, couldn't feel anything," West Sr. recalls of the fateful night. "I don't wish that on nobody."

For four months in 1988, he lay motionless in a hospital bed at Lafayette General Hospital. On Christmas Eve, he was visited by a group of women offering prayer.

"Some ladies came to my room and asked me what salvation means, what it means to be saved," West Sr. remembers. "They just kept going around my bed, going around my bed. It felt like I was floating above my bed."

Soon after the women left, his Christmas gift came.

"On Christmas Eve, that night, there was a loud voice. I never heard a voice like that in all my life. It was so loud it hurt my ears. I rose up to see what was going on, but my neck was still broken. No way I was supposed to wake up.

"My fiancé, she was sleeping. I didn't even see her come in. When I rose up, I was looking all around, then I went back to sleep. I'm thinking it was a dream. So the next morning, I ask if she can get up to see if my right leg was moving.

"It *was* moving!

"They (the nurses and doctors) thought I was having spasms. God was showing a way, when the doctor told me I never could walk again. The same doctor that told me that, when he saw me moving my legs, he got on his knees and started crying."

Jesse still was not able to walk, but the feelings and movement that appeared at Christmas suggested the real possibility of him being able to stand up and move again.

West Sr.'s journey was just beginning. The road to recovery would be as dangerous as that road he was traveling on that fateful night in 1988. There were surgeries to be done and rehab to endure, all at Charity Hospital in New Orleans – a third-world war zone of misery if ever there was one.

West Sr. remembers clearly the night someone attempted to set the hospital on fire.

"I'm on the seventh floor; my neck is still broken. I could still move, but my neck was still broken. All I could see was smoke.

"They had this RN that was with the handicapped people, the paraplegics, quadriplegics and stuff. She said she could walk and we couldn't, so she left us."

A few months after that nightmare, Jesse was robbed by a fellow patient who stole all the money his mom left for him in his nightstand.

Jesse explains, "I was just eighteen. I told my mom not to leave no money in my drawer. So he (another patient, an older gentleman) rolls to me and takes my money. I cried like a baby, because nobody does that to Jesse West."

While God was working in Jesse's life, it was a work in progress. Those verses about loving your enemies and turning the other cheek weren't quite set in yet.

"It (the theft) motivated me to get better, to start picking up weights. One night, they (the nurses) forgot to put the railing up on my bed. I knew how to get out and into my wheelchair. That night, I just locked my wheelchair and went to work. I broke everything he had in his mouth."

Weeks and months spent in 'Big Charity' hardened Jesse. Still it never would prepare him for the event that would cause him to flee the place forever.

"We had this nurse. Her name was Bernadine. She would sit in our dorm and give us medicine and everything. We were seven men in one room.

"This guy comes in with a brown paper bag; we're thinking like he was coming to give us some food, or it was her boyfriend or whatever. This guy pulls a gun. It was the first time I'd ever saw someone killed in front of me. He shot the nurse several times, then he pulled the gun on me – but, 'click', he had no bullets. He did that to all seven of us in that room.

"We couldn't move out the beds. The rails were up, and there was no way to put them down. We were in shock.

This poor lady was just bleeding. She couldn't catch her breath."

Jesse hoped he wouldn't have to stay in hell to find out if God was going to continue his miracle.

"They gave me a weekend pass. I was supposed to go back, but I went ask Tim to take me please, and Tim was the one that showed me how to walk."

Fontenot remembers his special patient.

"When I heard he wanted me to do his PT (physical therapy), I was very honored," recalls Dr. Tim, who still sees him as a patient today. "The only thing was Medicaid would not pay for his PT at my office so I saw him for free and figured if I would take care of him, God would take care of me... and He has."

Today, Jesse stands tall. He walks with the aid of a cane – his hand, still gnarled from the accident, wraps around the head of the cane in a custom fit. His shaved head reveals a small bump that covers a button placed underneath by doctors. It is evidence of another major health challenge in his life – a brain tumor he had to fight at the age of 16.

"I went through radiation for a month. I had to throw up like a pregnant woman. The tumor was like an orange inside my head. They put a button inside my head.

Whenever I catch a headache, I press the button and it goes away."

For all the man has been through, he has every reason in the world to want to take it easy, either through fear, exhaustion or entitlement. But Jesse stays active as he can, as all the reasons in the world don't compare to the promise he made to the One not of this world.

"I was a quadriplegic. If I quit moving, if I don't do anything, I'll be back in the wheelchair. That's why I try to stay working. I told God that if he blessed me to walk, I will work. So I will work."

Jesse West has kept his promise. He voluntarily took himself off of disability. According to Dr. Tim, West Sr. has studied to become a nurse's aide, earned a CDL license to become a truck driver, and currently is working on becoming an electrician.

CHAPTER SIX

We Had Food Attached

Watching Tim and Jacob Fontenot coordinate the mammoth weeklong event that is Tee Cotton, it is fascinating to see the father-and-son tandem work in sync. When talking about the bowl, the two men bounce ideas off each other like schizophrenic racquetballs in an overclocked clothes dryer. As the discussions deepen, eyes explode with the brightness of flash grenades; Cajun tongues grow thicker while words flow in fast-forward.

With the dynamics of their brainstorming sessions so strong, it's hard to imagine a bit over a decade ago when Jacob was just a young grasshopper and not yet a full-fledged partner in the endeavor.

But even the high school edition of Dr. Tim's son needs to be given proper credit. While the TCB bulb did first appear his dad's head in 1999, it was little Jacob that flicked the light switch.

Timbo (Cajun shorthand for *Tim's boy*) was just a high school junior back then, attending Sacred Heart and playing football for the Trojans. After a particularly rough 39-13 loss to the rival Bulldogs, he turned to his dad and said, "I hate to say this... I know we got whipped, but that was the funnest game of the year."[23]

"I saw that," Dr. Tim remembers the response he gave his son. "The Ville Platte High kids were real humble when they won; the Sacred Heart kids were real gracious when they lost. The atmosphere was great. People were even cooking barbecue."

And with that little exchange, the smallest of snowballs began to roll off the right side of Dad's brain.

"We asked, 'Wouldn't it be special, with the Ville Platte Cotton Festival, which the game usually occurs around, if we buy some Cotton Bowl patches for the jerseys for that game, the city championship?'" Dr. Tim questioned that same year.

"The people said, 'That costs a lot of money!'"

---

[23] Yes, he really did say 'funnest.'

"I said, 'Well, what about a trophy – not a little dinky trophy, but something that takes two hands to hold, like a Stanley Cup? Something you can hold over your head. That's when we came up with the 'Tee Cotton Bowl' – the *Little Cotton Bowl.*"

With the brainstorm, Dr. Tim commissioned his office manager, Gayle Fontenot (no relation) with the task of hunting down such a trophy.

"I walked in one morning and he said, 'I need you to find a big silver bowl,'" Gayle recollects. "And back then there was no DSL. It was dial-up Internet. Tim was like, 'I don't care how long it takes you to find one. Get me a silver bowl!'"

The request for a sports-related scavenger hunt was of no surprise to the office manager, who works in a small building that practically doubles as its own sports museum. Gayle's work area and the adjacent waiting room is plastered with framed photos and newspaper clippings referencing Ville Platte High, Sacred Heart, McNeese State University, and the New Orleans Saints. Examination rooms contain shelves overstuffed with football helmets, autographed equipment, and even rugby gear.

If the office doubles as a mini-museum, it also triples as a mini-chapel.

Gayle explains that the office staff will get together and pray, "Whenever something is going on with one of our patients, one of our family members.

"There are a couple of patients that will say, 'We love coming. It's like going to church.' It's a daily thing."

"(Tim) just tells everybody, 'We'll give God the glory, and we'll take the results,'" she says.

It's her boss' philosophy on not only patient care, but also practically everything else in life he encounters.

"I think he kind of takes it from the Apostle Paul," says Dr. Tim's physical therapy aide, Tyler Saucier. "Paul says 'I've become all things to all men.' I think Tim really takes that to heart."

Saucier, a former youth pastor now studying in the Baptist seminary – in addition to working for Tim – knows of his boss' penchant for bringing God to work daily.

See, before Tyler was an employee, he was a patient.

"Once, I'd cut part of my finger off. I went there (Fontenot Physical Therapy). He talked to me about God. I talked to him about God. We kind of just fed off each other."

While two people rooted in their own separate denominational worlds actually talking about faith and finding common ground to agree on can seem like an idealistic pipe dream, the laid-back attitude of Cajun culture helps everyone open their hearts and drop their guard just a bit more, even Christians.

"I know when I was a (Baptist) youth pastor, we'd work with Assembly of God churches, Christ Cathedral… and we'd work pretty well together," Tim's helper remarks. "A lot of times, the Catholic Church does its own thing, but in our community, we work with them, too. That's the good thing about south Louisiana. People just love people so much.

"It's all about putting it on the line. It's not about changing people's denominations. It's about loving them where they are."

The staff's behind the scenes contributions to the TCB are too plentiful to name, but the long to-do list all started with the office manager being able to snag the cup that would eventually become the Jerome Vidrine Memorial Trophy.

Via the Internet, Gayle was able to locate the perfect hyper-sized chalice in a store in New York City. The shop she purchased from existed just a block or so away from what would soon be referred to in the history books as Ground Zero.

In speaking of America's touchstone tragedy, it should be noted that a mere few weeks stood between 9/11 and TCB II. The events surrounding the second Tee Cotton Bowl, meant to honor police and firefighters with patriotic displays and activities, helped form the blueprint for the game as it is known today.

That year, 2001, also marked the official promotion of *Timbo* from being just 'Tim's kid' into the good doctor's full-fledged partner in crime.

"We had your article, where you wrote that you didn't think life in small-town America existed," The elder Fontenot says, referring to the column this author penned for the Opelousas *Daily World* after TCB II (and further explained in the preface). "A Dukes of Hazzard/ Mayberry kind of place. …You said you didn't think it existed until tonight."

The column, 'Tee Cotton II Brings Community Together', started off the first of what would be a zillion dinner table daydreams between the father and the son.

"We started looking (and saying), 'Yeah, this is sort of special.' Then we started talking. We sat around the dinner table one time…"

Jacob interrupts his dad to complete the thought.

"We just kind of fed off each other," he says. "Somebody brings something up, then it starts growing to a whole 'nother level."

Pulling senior rank, Dr. Tim bumps himself right back in the conversation.

"We said, 'This is a good story,'" the good doctor mentions. "We said, 'Who'd we want to tell our story to? ESPN? Sports Illustrated? Who'd we want the most?'"

The two decided that the TCB bug should first land in the ear of NFL Films.

The Fontenots soon learned that setting a sight on a fantasy pick in one thing; pulling the trigger is a different story.

High on adrenaline and low on experience, the duo set their plan of action on how to best impress the New Jersey media Mecca.

"I said, 'I don't want to write about me,'" Dr. Tim explained.

Due to his dad's modesty, it was decided that Jacob would be the scribe of record. He grabbed a pen and some unlined paper.

The handwritten note went into a care package of sorts. The box also contained a copy of the Daily World column, a Tee Cotton Bowl t-shirt, a swamp pop CD, homemade beef jerky, some tasso[24], and a *Chick-Can* apparatus used by locals for cooking the delicacy best known as 'drunken chicken'.

The parcel went off as excitement and then antagonizing anticipation set in. While waiting for a response, days turned to weeks, weeks to months, and months into fading hopes.

"Dad had pretty much just given up," notes Jacob.

But all it takes is one phone call.

Dr. Tim remembers the telephone conversation like it was yesterday.

"This is David Swain," he imitates the conversation in a *not-from-here* accent. "I'm a director from NFL Films. I got this anonymous letter…"

"Now we didn't sign it," Fontenot recollects, slipping back into his usual Cajun tones. "We just put 'If you need information, call Tim Fontenot, (then-Sacred Heart coach) Keith Menard, of call (then-Ville Platte High coach) Ward Courville.

"He says, 'The game intrigues us. Ya'll really call off school for Squirrel Day?'

"I said, 'Yeah. We can't play the game on Friday. Nobody would show up!'"

---

[24] A spicy smoked Cajun ham

Swain, a senior producer for NFL Films with over two decades' experience, remembers the first conversation he had with the founder.

"Dr. Tim's devotion to the game and that passion showed through the letter like a pure light of unshakeable belief," he explains. "Steve Sabol, the president of NFL Films, gave me the letter for a follow-up phone call. Dr. Tim was so engaging and interesting on the phone that we thought the story would be perfect for our yearly Thanksgiving show – which featured positive stories of giving."

The call from Swain for inclusion in the *NFL Films Presents* anthology was a minor miracle in itself. The filmmakers only pick one or two prep stories per year to document, and turn away an average of 20 stories for each one they select.

So, what made the Tee Cotton story so special for Swain's gang?

"A couple of things make the Tee Cotton Bowl unique," the producer says. "One was the difference between the two schools. One was a Catholic, primarily white and affluent school. The other school was predominantly African-American and facing a lot of economic and social challenges. The fact that the two squads could join together as they do in sharing and honoring each other spoke volumes about the power of the Tee Cotton Bowl event."

Swain goes on to describe another big selling point for Tee Cotton – location, location, location.

"The other element that made the story so attractive to us was the setting and the culture. Since college, when I had a friend named Alex Thibodeaux from Lafayette, Louisiana, I've been intrigued by Cajun culture. I've always loved the music and the food and I wanted to find out more about the people and what made them unique. The kind of solidarity that the population showed underscored the positive communal nature of the game."

As eloquent as David Swain's explanation was for choosing to feature the Tee Cotton Bowl, the founders of the event have a more down-to-earth theory as to the media's attention to the game.

"I said Jacob, it's a miracle. How'd we pull it off?" Dr. Tim questioned his son at the time.

"He said, 'Dad, it was handwritten and we had food attached!'"

If there was a time for the NFL Films to come on over, 2002 was it. The year marked the debut of the Tee Cotton Dream Bowl radio *tour-de-force* cooked up by Dr. Tim and Randy Guillory from KVPI. The guest speaker for the banquet would be LSU legend, NFL Pro-Bowler, and Sports Illustrated cover boy Tommy Casanova. Adding to the atmosphere would be the game's date – October 11 – a few days into Cajun Passover and the same week as the town's annual Cotton Festival.

Ville Platte was definitely ready for its close-up. The calendar date had been long circled by squirrels, senior producers, and super legends.

But like any hyped-up party, there's always an uninvited guest that tries to barrel their way into the fun.

Unfortunately, this crasher's name was Lili.

As in *Hurricane* Lili.

On October 3, 2002, a little more than a week before the game and – to add insult – the Thursday before squirrel season, the storm rolled into Louisiana with all the subtlety of a Lady Gaga encore. Sounding harmless as she wore her Category One label to the Louisiana shores, Lili was a tempest with the soul of a street fighter. By the time she got through with the Pelican State, over a quarter-million were without power. She filled the land with a half-foot of rainfall and storm surges of 12 feet. Her gusty rage shut down oil rigs and slapped the sugar cane crops like a nun chastising a child full of cuss words.

She even ran off without saying goodbye, leaving

Louisiana with the tab for her wanton ways – roughly $800 million in damages.

Lili left her autograph all over Ville Platte with every downed tree and snapped power line. It took five days for most of Ville Platte to be back on the power grid.

Too bad for the bad girl; she should have known that it would take a bit more than a federally-declared natural disaster to stop a party in Acadiana.

The head coaches for each school did whatever was necessary to be sure there would still be a show come Friday night.

Keith Menard, the head coach for SHS in 2002, was faced with not only preparing his athletes for the game but with preparing Soileau-Landry Stadium for the spectacle.

"I told our guys that if this thing comes through, I'll see whoever can make it here on Saturday (October 5, 2002)," he remembers telling his athletes.

"We had guys showing up with chain saws, kids with four-wheelers, all dragging off branches, trying to clear around the stadium" that was scheduled to host TCB II.

"My house was walking distance from the stadium. We were fortunate that we didn't have home damage, but we didn't have power, either."

To take care of his own family, Menard booked his

way to Baton Rouge to pick up a chain saw and a generator, with his family roughing their way through the week in a camper set up next to their home.

Also lucking out in his quest to find a generator – a device scarcer than snipe and more valuable than either gold bouillon or good boudin during hurricane season – was Ville Platte High's head coach at the time, Ward Courville.

With a bit of help from both his generator and his cell phone, Coach Courville made sure that Lili didn't wreck his calendar.

He used his portable power to run the VPH scoreboard against DeQuincy High in the days leading up to the TCB, and his cell to let his kids know that a *Cat I* wouldn't be enough to stop the show.

"You want to get the word out that you wanted to play," he recalls of his impromptu phone tree that helped re-organize his troops.

With the coaches taking care of their soldiers, all Dr. Tim needed to do to put the TCB train back on track was to use a bit of Cajun ingenuity… and eats.

"Tuesday (before the game), we're cooking at the Sacred Heart pavilion. All the people's freezers are going bad. People are busy trying to get the field ready. Ville Platte's making a celebration out of it! They're emptying their freezers and cooking a sauce by car light underneath the pavilion."

Once Swain found out about the determination of the town in the face of crisis, he was hooked.

"Hurricane Lili added another compelling layer to the story," the NFL Films producer notes. "It underscored the ability of the people of Ville Platte to come together and succeed despite difficult circumstances – whether they were manmade or natural. The resilience of the people in the face of the storm and its aftermath became another metaphor for the unique togetherness of the community."

He continues by remarking, "That part of Louisiana (Ville Platte) is not typical of the South. Because of the Cajun heritage, the people are unique and unlike any other place I've visited. They have a way of life and a way of living together that I thought of as 'Cajun Soul', and that is a very good thing and heartwarming way of life."

When NFL Films came to document this 'Cajun Soul' shining in the midst of Lili's aftermath, they came first class. The senior producer brought his Cadillac filmmakers with him, a crew that included cinematographers Donald Marx and David Dart – a duo with almost a half-century's experience between them. Together, Swain estimates Marx and Dart have shot around 2,200 NFL games.

Two separate camera teams shot 37 rolls of film, and leaving about 60 minutes of footage on the cutting room floor for each minute that made it onto the final product.

"Normally, we shoot at a ratio of about 20 to 1," mentions Swain. "But there were so many compelling interviews; background material from both school and game events and Cajun cultural elements that we wanted to cover – we were compelled to shoot more."

And for all the time the crew was in Ville Platte, they managed surprisingly to stay in the shadows.

"During practices, they hid themselves really well," VPH coach Courville remembered of what he called an "out of this world" event.

"It was kind of surreal," the ex-head coach recalls.

"Not even J.T. Curtis[25] from John Curtis had been on ESPN for a 15-minute segment before."

With every repeat of the feature over the years come increments of notoriety for Courville and the others featured in film.

"I've had people come up years later and they will say, 'Hey, I saw you on TV,' and I'll be like, 'They're still playing that thing?'" the former Bulldog coach jokes.

---

[25] Head coach of John Curtis Christian High School in River Ridge, La. and Louisiana Sports Hall of Fame member. J.T. Curtis, still active, has amassed 23 state titles in his career at the school his father founded.

Coach Menard, formerly of Sacred Heart, remembers how even "one of our team doctors (Dr. Chuck Aswell) was recognized at a cardiology convention in Florida."

But if anyone still has yet to escape the limelight that the ESPN feature has brought, it would have to be the father of the TCB himself.

Dr. Tim recalls a visit to Huntsville, Texas with Jacob in 2004 to cheer on McNeese State against Sam Houston State. It was a game that sticks out for two reasons: a bunch of trucks on the roadside, and a goat on the sidelines.

"We had some guys sitting behind us – they were just college guys from Sam Houston enjoying the game. I asked them, 'What's with the goat?'"

After a plausible explanation that the animal was a tradition trotted onto the field after scores, Tim had to ask about all the vehicles on the side of the road.

"I say, 'Hey man, is it hunting season out here?'"

"They say, 'Yeah, that's why we have all the cars and all the people.'"

"I say, 'We hunt squirrels in our hometown.'"

"They went, 'Yeah, we saw this thing on TV about these two schools in Louisiana, how they don't play on Squirrel Day...'

After a slight and befuddled pause, the students begin to crack up laughing.

"I remember you!" they exclaimed. "You're that guy that's on ESPN!"

While Dr. Tim's not one for recognition or accolades, if they must be had, he'd prefer to receive the compliments during a Saturday afternoon then in the wee hours.

"One time we (Tim and *Timbo*) were on a trip. The phone starts ringing at two in the morning. It's one of Jacob's buddies – 'Hey, I'm in a sports bar! Your dad's on TV!'"

As with most everything, fame fades. The challenge to be seized in such a moment as the NFL Films feature is to create something that lasts longer than the blink of Warhol's eyelid.

Such a long-term bond is exactly what has happened between Dr. Tim and David Swain. They still speak with each other several times a year, in an association initiated by Fontenot.

Food, of course, was involved.

"In 2004, we actually brought some crawfish and sausage to NFL Films," Fontenot speaks about a surprise trip he and Jacob took to New Jersey, a year after the feature made its tour of satellite dishes and coaxial cables.

"We arrived unannounced. I knew David Swain would

be there. Steve Sabol was there, but I didn't get a chance to meet him. He was in a meeting.

"We get to the front. Huge place. Jacob said, 'Oh dad, my knees are weak.'

"I said, 'Take off your shoes; we're on holy ground.'

"We go in. They have this huge wall. They have a big wall of like 100 Emmys. The lady at the front, she's like 'Well, who are you here to see?'

"David Swain, please.

"So she calls. 'Tim Fontenot here to see you.'

After a second or two of silence, the crasher added, "I said, 'Tell him Dr. Tim.'

"I can hear him start laughing, and then she starts smiling.

"He walks up and (boisterously asks), 'Why are you here?'

"I said, 'To bring you some sausage and crawfish.'

"No really?

"Yeah, really!

Swain gladly confirms the story, even if it causes a stomach growl or two.

"I believe that Tim has been to NFL Films twice and we're always thrilled to have him – especially because food is always involved!"

CHAPTER SEVEN

Tim Brings the Umbrella

In August of 2004, a few months before TCB IV, Dr. Tim received possibly the biggest piece of fan mail he could ever hope for.

The letter read:

Dear Mr. Fontenot,

His Holiness Pope John Paul II has received your kind letter and enclosures, and he has asked me to thank you in his name.

His Holiness was pleased to learn of the annual Tee Cotton Bowl held in Ville Platte. He offers prayerful good wishes that this event will inspire lasting friendships, foster a spirit of mutual respect and cooperation in the pursuit of excellence, and strengthen solidarity and harmony in the larger community.

Upon all taking part in the competition the Holy Father cordially invokes God's blessings of joy and peace.

Bureau Chief

Monsignor Valention Di Cerbo

The notice of official Papal blessings was the result of nothing more than Dr. Tim crying one more time into the wilderness, hoping for one more response of validation for his project.[26]

The Papal blessings marked three straight years of remarkable recognition for the then-five year old game. The NFL Films spectacle of 2002 and the acknowledgment from

---

[26] In the package sent out to the Vatican, there was no tasso or bizarre devices to cook down-home drunken fowl. There was, however, a copy of the NFL Films feature and a Tee Cotton visor. Could the visor possibly be a gift to complement the sunglasses given to the Pope by rock star Bono during their meeting on famine relief? One can imagine the Pontiff scurrying around the Vatican in his downtime sporting the accessories and slyly, joyously grinning.

His Holiness in 2004 helped sandwich the second jewel of the early-years trifecta – a $10,000 gift from the Louisiana *United Way* and *Parade* magazine in 2003.

The check, a top prize for winning the *Louisiana Community Quarterback* award sponsored by the two entities, was presented in front of a December Superdome crowd there to see the Saints topple the Dallas Cowboys, 27-13.

Memories of the event lasted a lot longer than the money, which Fontenot immediately divided between the two schools he'd taken under his wing.

"One of Jacob's teammate's classmate's mothers worked for City Hall," Tim details as he recalls the origins of the contest entry. "Her husband and I were classmates, too. She says, 'I want to nominate you for an award.'"

Fontenot, not one to seek personal recognition, originally refused the idea. The friend, Nina David,[27] did sway his mind once she mentioned the bucket of bucks that came with the Community Quarterback honor. Dr. Tim began to see the award as an opportunity to raise money for the Tee Cotton schools, and eventually agreed.

"So she nominated us," the founder remembers. "We're one of the finalists, and I'm like, 'Cool.' We get up

---

[27] *DAH-veed*

there and there's like the Girl Scouts and all these big agencies we're up against."

The big agencies, however, were no match for small town football.

Soon enough, Dr. Tim was in the end zone during the Saints-Cowboys pre-game activities, smiling for the grip-and-grin paparazzi and lifting a replica check as big as he was. With the win, Tim kept his promise to split the cash prize between the two schools. According to Fontenot, Sacred Heart put their share towards a new ticket booth while Ville Platte High took in enough scratch for new uniforms.

The game just keeps growing. Newfound ties to the Maxwell Football Club have given fresh avenues for the TCB to again be recognized on a national level for its contributions to prep pigskin. Over the years, the accolades have just kept coming.

As the Tee Cotton Bowl is nothing if not a singular tale of faith and football woven into one strong cloth, the nods have come from both textiles.

On the faith side of the equation, the *Win a Day of Uncommon Service with Tony Dungy* award given to the Tee Cotton teams in 2009 continued to bring legitimacy to the TCB as a true Christian event. The honor, the result of a contest sponsored by Tyndale House Publishers to celebrate the release of Dungy's *Uncommon* book, also gave the bowl a major stamp of approval from the Protestant community.

"The purpose of this contest was to show and tell others about the uncommon heroes all around us that are making a difference, sometimes one person at a time," explained Yolanda Sidney, senior marketing manager for Tyndale House, as to the criteria used to select a winner.

"These heroes are daring to be uncommon, which means they dare to be more like Jesus – in character – in every part of their life, at home, work, school, church, or in their community. The two high schools were very uncommon heroes in our eyes."

The *Uncommon* event also presented undisputable evidence as to how much trust Fontenot has in both the TCB and in the power of prayer.

"I knew we were going to win," Dr. Tim says in reflection without a hint of bravado or pride. "In fact, I didn't schedule any appointments for that week (that the winning entrants were scheduled to meet Tony Dungy as part of the prize). I said that I'm going to pray that we were going to win."

Wasn't it a huge risk for Fontenot to clear out his schedule months in advance, in hopes of winning a nationwide contest?

The Tee Cotton founder just smiles at the thought and says, "If I'm going to pray for rain, I'm going to bring an umbrella."

While Dr. Tim had a certain feeling that he and the coaches were going to take that trip to Indianapolis, VPH coach Serie and SHS coach Wall had no idea they would be boarding that plane to meet the NFL coaching legend/ broadcast analyst/ best-selling author.

Of course, it would have helped for them to know that they were entered in the contest.

As former coaches Menard and Courville were blindsided with the news of NFL Film's interest in 2002, current head coaches Wall and Serie were kept in the dark until the day the Uncommon winner was announced.

Just chalk it up to another one of Fontenot's surprise 'Christmas presents' the schools have had to grow accustomed to.

Coach Serie of VPH was ambushed with the good news while at his school's athletic banquet.

"We were having our awards ceremony," he explains, "when he called me and said, 'Coach, we're going to be flying out to visit Tony Dungy.'

"I said, 'Dr. Tim, you've got to be kidding me.' I couldn't believe it.

"If someone else would've told me, I'd been 'ahhh', but with Dr Tim, it's like 'Yeah, that's something he would do.'"

As amazed as Serie was with the news, he was even more surprised with the humbleness of their celebrity host.

"When we met (Dungy), I was expecting to see an entourage, him coming in very sophisticated; but he came in very nonchalantly… tennis shoes… real casual."

Coach Wall of Sacred Heart picked up on the same laid-back vibes from the Super Bowl-winning coach, even as he was able to take in some advice from the NFL figure.

"Tony – what helps him – is he's a Christian man," the SHS leader recalled most from the visit. "He's got a son playing in high school; he knows the problems we have.

"He's a real family man. He reminded us how important it is to spend time with family. He had lost a son. I don't think he had guilty feelings, he just knows how important it is to spend that time. He taught us that it's not important, the wins and losses. It's important how we treat our family and our fellow coaches."

During the weekend visit, the Cajun contingent were treated to a tour of the Colts' facilities, Butler University (filming location for the *Hoosiers* movie and a previous host for USA vs. Russia basketball) and Riley Children's Hospital.

The visit to the hospital was of special importance, both to fulfill the 'Service' part of the 'Uncommon Service' award, and to help draw attention to the *Baskets of Hope* children's hospital charity.[28]

While the dream weekend lasted much shorter than the Ville Platte posse would have liked, the visit did allow for some good-natured ribbing, although at the expense of someone not in attendance.

A Mr. Peyton Manning, to be more specific.

Tim Fontenot told Dungy of the 1993 2A Louisiana State Championship baseball game between Sacred Heart and Isidore Newman High School of New Orleans. The good doctor was a trainer for the Trojans; Jacob, a batboy. As the story goes, Peyton – then a shortstop for the Newman Greenies – allowed the ball to run right under him. The

---

[28] Tony Dungy is the national spokesperson for the *Baskets of Hope* charity. More information can be found at *www.basketsofhope.org*.

grounder, sailing betwixt his ankles, gave Sacred Heart the go-ahead run which led to a 5-4 win and the 2A hardware.

"(Dungy) cracked up," according to Tim, in storyteller guise. "He had a belly laugh, then he texted Peyton."

With the weekend of bonding came an invite for Coach Dungy to speak to the Tee Cotton kids for the 2009 banquet. Although unable to make the event, he did send a personalized recorded message for the teams.

It was a shame that the coach could not personally make the event that year. As the first African-American coach to win the Super Bowl and an outspoken Christian, he'd seem to be a perfect fit to speak at the annual dinner's longstanding themes of race and faith.

Dungy would have been in great company, too, as the annual affair has previously attracted such notables in the sports world as wrestler 'Big Cat' Ernie Ladd; Louisiana legend Tommy Casanova; Los Angeles Dodger Danny Ardoin; and elite Super Bowl referee Greg Gautreaux.

For the athletes and coaches involved in the Tee Cotton Bowl, the night-before dinner arguably overshadows the game, itself.

"The atmosphere is very intimate," warns Dr. Tim. "It's intimate the way you talk about things you wouldn't talk about to anybody else. We talk about race; we talk about God; we talk about emotions.

"These kids kneel down and they pray for the guy who's going against him to have their best game. You're not praying for yourself – you're praying for the other guy. That means you've got to get better. That's a powerful thing."

The 'powerful thing' Dr. Tim speaks about comes from Proverbs 27:17. "Iron sharpens iron," he quotes from the passage. "When you do that, you make each other better. That's how you honor God."

"Iron sharpens iron" is the basis for the way the bowl game is played; the Bible verse is the tagline on TCB tee shirts given to the athletes on both squads.

The quote embodies the mission statement the athletes must make as they prepare for Tee Cotton Week – to be sure your rival is at the top of his game, so you are forced to be at the top of yours.

Even though the Proverb is the Tee Cotton Bowl's statement, the verse leads to a question each and every football player must answer:

"Can you play that hard where you leave your soul on the field?"

For a decade, Fontenot has placed this interrogatory in front of every athlete to attend the banquet. It is a question that may have been reworded or rephrased from time-to-time, but has never been remolded or watered down.

In an event that weaves faith and football into one cloth, that question runs the loom.

Just as half the Tee Cotton cloth is faith, half the game's participants are from a public school – the perfect recipe for an ACLU attorney just waiting to earn his or her paycheck or face time in the news.

Yet, as the event enters its second decade, legal challenges to the game and its message have been nil.

"We always follow the line," Dr. Tim notes of the tightrope he knows he must walk. "We always have the banquet at Sacred Heart the night before, when we talk about God. For the pre-game, we always have a student say the prayer.

"If they want to fire me, fire me!" Tim jokes. "Cut my salary," laughs the Tee Cotton Bowl's biggest volunteer.

Jumping back into a more serious mode, Fontenot says he doesn't know "if the public school doesn't appreciate it more."

Perhaps they do.

"That's what makes (the Tee Cotton Bowl) so special," remarks Ville Platte High quarterback Cody Jones.

"You really don't see too many public high schools getting into the religious thing. When you go to a Catholic high school for the banquet, it just makes it more recognized."

Fellow teammate Jesse James West Jr. agrees that bringing religion to the field is a good thing. "Not too many people would do that," he mentions. "We are a small town; we all come together as blood."

Bulldog head coach Serie has noticed the quiet but steady evolution of the Tee Cotton as a Christian event.

"Honestly, I've never heard one complaint," he notes. "When we first started, religion wasn't a thing. It was like, 'There's your religion; there's my religion.' I think now it's starting to come where it's a very sincere moment when we get together the night before. We're really praying together more for each other now than in the earlier years."

It's easy to cheer for Fontenot and the Tee Cotton concept if one is a participant in and benefactor of the spectacle. A prayer or two might seem to be an appropriate price of admission for an athlete or coach to be part of the phenomenon.

But what about those whose battle is not with the team across the tracks but – potentially – with the attorneys across the state and country?

Toni Hamlin is the Evangeline Parish Superintendent of Schools. A diminutive, well-spoken woman, she comes across as a stick of explosive dynamite delicately wrapped in a coat of Southern charm. Her voice resonates in coquettish tones that can disarm in earnest hospitality one moment, cut like the sharpest petal in a bouquet of steel magnolias the next.

The possibility of outside 'civil liberty' threats disrupting the Tee Cotton Bowl bother the leader but little.

"We're not advocating religion," she insists. "Know that."

To her, Dr. Tim's knack for bringing God to the gridiron is anything but a liability. His enthusiasm is welcomed.

On the founder's mannerisms, she says, "We're talking about a spirit you portray as a model person. I think there are just certain qualities that people have."

She compares her public school's TCB participation with those of other schools around the nation that recognize 'Around the Flagpole'-type activities. 'Flagpole' guidelines help set up the rules-of-thumb for the week.

"The ruling as I understand it, and have understood it for several years, is that if you have a club at school, let's say a Christian club. The only restriction you have with that –

and even with our prayer – is it cannot be teacher led. It can be student led.

"I am very comfortable, legally, in that aspect. We are not teaching a religion; we are teaching good sportsmanship and the respect of others. I've never heard one comment, one complaint."

There are many in the town who pray, literally, that she never will.

CHAPTER EIGHT

Sacred Heart Becomes Sacred Ground

"... Just a good ol' boys
Never meaning no harm..."
– Waylon Jennings

In the Daily World sports column from 2001, entitled "Tee Cotton II Brings Community Together", Ville Platte was admirably compared to fictional Hazzard County, the setting for The *Dukes of Hazzard* TV show. The laid-back lifestyle, the camaraderie of rural-minded residents, the do-it-yourself attitude all ring true in both the fantasy and factual locales.

With a setting so similar in spirit to the CBS classic, it was only a matter of time before the town would raise its own version of a Duke boy.

Enter Cade McDaniel, the Sacred Heart MVP of the 2007 Tee Cotton Bowl and member of the 2010 Trojan senior class.

While Cade was not one to be "In trouble with the law since the day he was born" like Bo and Luke, the standout Trojan athlete could manage to be every bit as rascal as any wild-eyed Southern boy, fictional or non.

A good example of Cade's mischief was the time in high school that he was playing hide-and-go-seek and managed to wedge himself in the smokehouse of a local store.

Of course, winding up stuck in the moment of a fevered game of hide-and-seek is one thing. Winding up in Texas on the day of one's religion final to buy a truck is another.

Yes, he skipped the test just like he'd skip the speed bumps in his school's parking lot with the red Toyota he bought that day.

By the way, when called on his aversion to said bumps by the principal, he politely explained his bad habit as the fault of his mother, Mitzi.

It wasn't the only time that Cade had his mother rolling her eyes or Sacred Heart school faculty earning their paychecks.

Teachers were kept perpetually occupied trying to determine if his work was his own or the labor of his female friends, who were usually too willing to help out – and usually too frustrated when he'd wind up getting higher scores than they did.

The SHS staff frequently wound up finding themselves on the receiving end of Cade's pranks. One of his more classic moves involved a time he was ordered to the office. SHS staff kept calling him to the office for fifteen minutes straight, only to find him hiding under a secretary's desk.

"Why ya'll keep calling me?" he questioned them, according to his mother's recollection of the story. "I'm in the office (like you asked). You just didn't say where in the office!"

McDaniel was simultaneously a piece of work and a work in progress.

"He was a kid that always had a smile on his face," remembers Tyler Saucier of Fontenot Physical Therapy, where Cade would go on Saturdays to get patched up from the dings that occurred under Friday night lights. "He was one of those cats that everybody just has fun with."

But on August 30, 2009, the unthinkable occurred. The boy who always brought life to Sacred Heart's 2010 senior class wound up fighting for his own.

Whereas Cade was the quintessential fun-loving Cajun boy unique to Louisiana, he was also the essence of teenagers everywhere in the United States, with too much access to alcohol and a false cloak of invincibility.

In the wee hours of that August morning, in a car piled with friends and driven by a seventeen year-old Ross Veillion, Cade's night out would end up in an operating room inside Lafayette General Hospital.

Alcohol was suspected as a factor in the crash, and among numerous charges brought against the driver was first-offense DWI.

After a fight for a bit over a week inside the hospital's Pediatric Intensive Care Unit, Cade would pass away on September 9, 2009.

The other five teenagers in the vehicle managed to escape with minor-to-moderate injuries according to news reports.

Mrs. McDaniel remembered their injuries as little more than a series of scratches and stitches.

"One girl had three stitches under her chin. Another girl had four teeth pushed back – she had braces, or they probably would have been knocked out."

"No severe injuries at all," added her husband, Todd, speaking in empty tones of disbelief.

The McDaniels' son would be the only one in the single-vehicle accident not to walk away.

For Cade's classmates, the initial news did not reveal the severity of the accident. They just believed this would be one more jam Cade would work himself out of.

"When we first heard about the accident, we were like – 'Cade? Aw, no!'" SHS quarterback Stuart Schexnayder recalls, giving a *"Here he goes again"* inflection to his voice.

"There goes Cade, having a good time. Then we realized the seriousness of the incident. We all got kind of worried. When we got to the hospital, we knew it was bad."

The parents' final days with their son were made much more comfortable with help from the hospital. Lafayette General provided the McDaniels with an empty patient room for their stay. The fact that Cade, 17, still qualified for a bed in the PICU meant far less restrictive visitation rules than if he would have landed in a regular Intensive Care Unit.

Schexnayder – Cade's classmate, teammate, and friend since childhood – used his quarterback instincts to help take charge. His leadership abilities did shine through as he helped the McDaniel family through their time at Lafayette General.

Mr. McDaniel remembers Stuart requesting permission for the senior class to keep the family company with footage of Cade's game play.

"So he called me and asked, 'Would you mind? We'd like to bring the TV and the DVD.

"He's the one that organized all of this (the visits by the senior class). Anything that he could do to help out, he was out to do it."

Stuart was just one person inside Cade's large network of friends. Cade's mother readily recalls that "it wasn't like he had to be around one person. (Cade) just floated around."

Still, it's hard to imagine stronger bonds than those that ran between the straight-laced Schexnayder and the Devil-may-care McDaniel.

The bonds, of course, were formed in gyms, on fields, and track ovals.

Even in tee ball, the boys' personalities began to emerge.

"If they hit the ball and Stuart was at third base, and Cade was in right field, Stuart would run all the way over to get the ball," Cade's dad recalls. "That's how aggressive he was."

Meanwhile, little Cade "was there tossing up the pine cones," oblivious to the play at hand, his mother smiles as she remembers.

The Odd Couple aspect of the two friends would manifest itself again in middle-school basketball.

Mitzi remembers one particularly frazzling trip she would take with her son and Stuart to an away game.

"One time they made the mistake to ride with me to Broussard[29] for a basketball game," she says with the beginnings of a smirk. "I had a little pull-down DVD player in my van. Well, I lose the caravan, and here's Stuart: 'Are we going to get there on time? Are we?'

"He was just so nervous. Then here's Cade just watching the movie not worried. I had to stop three or four places to ask for directions. When we finally got there, Stuart ran to him mom and said, 'Gimme two Tylenol,' he was so stressed out.

"(Meanwhile) Cade didn't even know we were lost."

---

[29] A town in Cajun country almost an hour's drive due south from Ville Platte.

Stuart best describes his easygoing, lifelong friend as the one who tried to keep everybody's spirits up.

"He kept everyone smiling. He kept making jokes. He was the guy wanting to make everybody happy."

The SHS team leader went on about his fallen classmate, mentioning, "He always had your back anytime you needed him."

Perhaps that quality is the singular reason that Cade could easily fit the description of a prototypical Cajun male or an honorary Duke cousin. Somewhere under the bit-too-rough exterior and sneaky grin was the heart of a guy who would always 'have your back.'

Stories of Cade sticking up for the little guy began to emerge in the hospital and right after his passing, as students and parents began to share stories with his mother.

"This lady, I had no idea who she was, said, 'I need to tell you something.' She said her son had some kind of disability and he was on the football team. She'd worry about him, so she'd go to practice every day. Cade walked up and asked her, 'Why do you come to practice every day?'

"She said, 'I like to watch my son because I worry about him.' She told Cade what kind of problems he had.

"So she said (other team members) had roughed him up a few days after she'd talked to Cade, and Cade said (to the teammates) that they'd better not touch him again. Cade really protected him.

"She said he couldn't play on the football team after Cade died, so he asked Coach Wall if he could become one of the trainers."

There was another tale Mitzi heard of where Cade was involved in a relatively ugly pranking of the freshmen by the senior class.

One of the ninth graders on the receiving end of the taunting told Cade's mom, "You know what? Two days before the accident he called me. He said, 'I'm sorry' and he apologized for being mean. I don't even know how we got my cell phone number."

For someone as unique and popular as Cade, it seemed only fair that even his death was larger-than-life.

Upon hearing of his passing, the Ville Platte High football team immediately broke practice to meet with Sacred Heart on their field to mourn and show support.[30]

Sacred Heart vice principal Dawn Shipp recalls the power of that visit.

"It's not something that's a performance they were putting on," she explains. "It was personal; it was intimate.

---

[30] See back cover photo.

When the Ville Platte High boys came to pray with our boys, it wasn't 'Hey, how ya doin?' They were hugging each other, embracing each other. They were crying. The coaches were crying with our coaches."

The same rivals that showed up at the Sacred Heart practice to help the Trojans grieve also showed at the funeral in their uniform jerseys.

"I was not exactly expecting it; just very happy to see it," noted Fr. Gene Tremie of Sacred Heart Catholic Church. "They sort of had a path to get through together.

"They wanted to express their sorrow with our young men. I was edified. Did I expect it? No, but once I saw it, I became very happy."

Schexnayder remembers the Bulldogs greeting his team with handshakes at the church.

"They were there for us. They came out and supported us. It's a team we've become close to over the past years through the Tee Cotton Bowl and stuff.

"The bonds are there because we are so close."

With several local Catholic schools from other parishes also attending the services, the crowd of mourners for the funeral was nothing short of overflow.

The Bulldogs continued their solidarity with the Trojans throughout the season, even adorning their helmets with white-on-black decals bearing Cade's jersey number, *20*. The emblems went up at their home game against Oakdale High on September 17. They'd remain on until after the Tee Cotton Bowl, the last game of the season.

Jennifer Vidrine, who helped organize the helmet sticker memorial, says, "It was the right thing to do. We had to do it. When I told the (Ville Platte) boys about it, they were like, 'Oh yes, Ms. Jennifer, we can't wait to do it.'

"They were ecstatic. They were too happy to honor him. There's a communion, a fellowship, a community out there to support each other."

Jesse James West Jr. of Ville Platte High summed up his teams support for Cade. Immediately after the Oakdale game, which the Bulldogs won 45-12, West said, "We're doing it for him right now. We were like brothers."

Across the railroad tracks on Soileau-Landry Field, the Trojans' first game without their wide receiver would solidify Cade's passing into nothing short of local legend.

McDaniel's body had been cremated. It was a decision, by happenstance, that Cade made for himself. One day while overhearing his mother and father discuss their own options for day we all must face, Cade jumped in the conversation and announced that cremation would be his choice, also.

Prior to the Trojans' game against the North Central Hurricanes on September 11 – a week before the helmet decal honor bestowed by Ville Platte High – Todd and Mitzi approached Coach Wall with a Ziploc bag and a wish.

If their son was not going to be playing on the field, he was going to become part of the field.

"We took a small portion of him and just showed up at the game, gave it to them (the senior football players) before the game. We'd checked with Coach Wall. They did it in a little private deal."

Friend and fellow Trojan athlete Ian David remembers the request to scatter Cade's ashes on the field.

"Just right before we ran out, (Cade's mom) said, 'Could you do this for us?' It was spur of the moment.

"He's just part of what we play on now. It's pretty much where he lived anyway. He lived for track and football, and now he's part of both. Now he's there."

While the act brought a measure of comfort to family and friends, it did defy – albeit innocently – official teachings of the Catholic Church.

The act was discreetly, quietly handled between the parents, the coach, and the football team. Not even Fr. Tremie was aware of the impromptu memorial at first.

But word began to spread – first to the community and then ultimately to the media. Once reporters arrived, it placed the priest in an awkward situation.

"No one told us it was going to happen," recalls the priest. "The Catholic Church teaches us that you should keep the remains in tact. People see movies and stuff and think it's okay to spread the ashes out. But we have the same respect for the remains as we would have for someone that is not cremated. It should be in tact.

"Because this happened without our knowledge, we didn't give permission for it. But it was on television. People thought this was an authorized event. I had to write an article and I gave the article to the coaches and the teachers. I put it in the bulletin and the newspaper. We brought to the funeral home the rules of the Catholic Church."

As surprised as the pastor was, he chose to use the moment as a time of teaching rather than chastisement. Instead of causing a rift, he seized the event to re-enforce Church teachings to those involved.

"The young men that did this, we don't see that they had ill will or that they knew they were doing something wrong. They just weren't informed. We tried to let them know why the Church teaches this. It's a chance for them to get to know the teachings at a time when they were really paying attention to it. We might have said it ten times before, but they wouldn't have absorbed it. We weren't condemning them; we wanted to instruct them. It was a good opportunity.

"At the school board meeting we said this is a horrible thing, the death of this young man. But God is drawing good from it, which is what He does."

Dr. Tim Fontenot, founder of the Tee Cotton, separately described very similar sentiments. Working closely with the athletes and friends of both schools, Dr. Tim was privy to the scuttlebutt of every rumor and reputation-maker Cade was involved with.

Fontenot sees how the power of Christ and the community helped the town heal after the accident.

"I think God said, 'Devil, I'm not going to let you have this one.' Cade may not have been an angel, but he just might be a saint."

Almost a year after Cade's death, visits to the house by Cade's friends are dwindling. It's an expected fear for Cade's mother, who talks about her worry of the 'Second Year', when those not inside the nuclear family begin to go on about their daily lives and stop checking on those most affected by a loss.

One person who will possibly break the Second Year cycle is, not surprisingly, Stuart.

"(Stuart) had called me the day before yesterday," Todd McDaniel says appreciatively in an interview conducted about ten months after his son's passing. "He came and spent about two hours. He talked to Mitzi. I can't describe how good he is. He'll send us messages and talk to us."

Today, inside the house on his family's soybean-and-rice farm, Cade's room sits untouched. Every trophy and honor sits on display proudly.

Somehow, in the clutter of awards, tributes, and newspaper clippings, three items beg to be noticed.

The first is a photo of a scoreboard of a game between the Trojans and the Blue Jays of St. Ed's of Eunice (La.). It announces an endgame score of 20-8, with the victory nod towards the Trojans. The numbers mean nothing more than the fact the SHS had a better night, until Mr. Todd begins to read between the lights.

The game occurred on September 4, 2009, in the middle of Cade's ordeal. Cade's dad explains that '20' was not only Sacred Heart's score that night, but also his son's jersey number. Eight, to hear the dad describe, represents September 8, the date Cade would be declared brain dead.

The numbers could be sheer coincidence, or a sign that Someone Else had His hand in this dark time and that peace that passes all understanding was there in the midst.

In another corner of the room sits an ornament as a *'Thank You'* from the Southern Eye Bank for Cade's donation of his eyes after his death.

Cade's mother was not aware he had even signed a donor card until the accident. It was just one more surprise from her son.

Lastly, in the room there is a small painting of a track runner. The artwork shows promise. After inquiring, Mr. Todd volunteers that the art is a creation of Cade's. It's a simple enough work, but still one that shows remarkable aesthetic potential, based on the color choices and illustration of movement.

Talent with a brush? One more little known fact about Cade hidden under his rascal reputation.

The father is asked if the painting was inspired by the son's love of track. After all, the son had been to the state meet for hurdles twice in the past, and was almost a shoo-in to qualify had he been alive for the 2010 championships.

"Not particularly. He took art because it was an easy class."

Typical Cade, no doubt.

CHAPTER NINE

Showtime

It's 3:30 p.m. on the day of Tee Cotton Bowl X. Dr. Tim and Jacob, fresh from their whirlwind pep rally visits, pull into the gates of Ville Platte High's stadium. They hold witness to the development of a virtual tent city surrounding the playing field. The swelling is especially rapid by the north end zone near the ticket booth. It is almost as if in the two-hour absence of the Fontenots, the National Guard arachnid-inspired tent resting behind the north goal post was busy giving birth to a host of smaller shelters, all competing for Mama's attention.

As his Suburban grinds to a halt, Dr. Tim immediately pops out of the vehicle to help move tables under the inflatable crimson tarantula. No words are spoken; no instructions are given. The good doctor just jumps out and starts grabbing and unfolding.

While Tim unloads, Joe Cahn continues his meandering adventure through the canopy maze. Nine hours after tailgating officially began, the Commish's appetite and cameras are still soaking up the Cajun flavor like a morning biscuit in red-eye gravy.

Crossing paths with Cahn and Fontenot is a much smaller spectator. He is a boy of no more than four years old. The wanderer wears a pint-sized Ville Platte jersey and a plastic New Orleans Saints replica helmet that hides not-so-sure eyes. The child recognizes a black-and-gold inflatable hat that resembles his garnishing the end zone. He breaks a smile as he gazes upon the icon. The structure is twice the boy's height and could easily double as the child's playroom. The child's smile lingers long enough for dad to take a picture.

Nearby, Jacob Fontenot looks around in relief. Pleased, he mentions that at this point, "We're just trying to put all the right chess pieces on the board."

As the son is making the reflection, Dad has disappeared again in yet another full-on insomniac hamster-on-Red Bull burst of manic energy. While Jacob contemplates, Dr. Tim checks on the new Hall-of-Fame inductees and gets an ETA on the arrival of the Southern University drum line. From the stands, the coordinator looks like the digitized ball from the world's biggest game of Pong, as he pops back-and-forth from end zone to end zone with increasing swiftness.

Doug Stanford, a member of the 'Cracked' pyro team that will be setting off the rockets' red glare come show time, rapidly receives his set of instructions from the good doctor.

"It's more elaborate than the D-Day invasion," Stanford laughs. His mood is quite jovial for a man handling explosives and wearing a shirt with a big 'X' on the back.

The only things moving faster than Dr. Tim at this point are the grains of *Slap Ya Mama* in the hourglass.[31] Sixty minutes lapse inside a blink during the orchestra of organized chaos.

During the fast-forward frenzy, Jacob Fontenot busies himself with checking on the 'Tee Tron' in the south end zone. The 'Tron will be used to roll highlights of all the

---

[31] *Slap Ya Mama* – like Tony Chachere's, another seasoning popular in Cajun country and used like salt or pepper.

yesteryears as soon as the sun goes down and darkness cooperates. He carefully adjusts the aim of the projector towards the huge white sheet that plasters the side of the moving van.

It may not be the punter's nightmare screen at the Dallas Cowboys' stadium, but at least its home.

While the Fontenots scramble, the first hundred or so Ville Platte High fans begin to find their way to the bleachers. Each early bird comes in clutching a paper boat of slow-roasted pulled pork from the day's featured cookout. In this neck of the woods, boucheries trump bobbleheads any day of the week as a pre-game enticement.

As if the aroma of the food doesn't already remind fans that this is a Louisiana football game, a 'Who Dat' sign quietly pops up in the stands.

Under the media tent, a few female volunteers reminisce about their 1970's high school glory years. They chat with each other about the archaic rules of association from 'back in the day'.

"When I grew up, if I had a boyfriend at Sacred Heart, he could not take me to prom... but he wouldn't be my boyfriend anyway, because they wouldn't associate with us," one of the ladies recalls as she checks on the gumbo and fried fish for the TCB VIP's.

"That's how far we've come. It (harmony between the schools) wouldn't have happened, at least not on this scale, without Dr. Tim. It's a calling from God."

In the background, the afternoon concert begins. On the track in front of the home side of the stadium, JJ and the Zydeco Dog Pound begin to percolate the backbeat to an infectious dance number

The ladies continue chatting, as Cajun ladies are wont to do. Dr. Tim has magically transported himself next to them, silently emptying box upon box of food for the courtesy tent. In the background, the Ville Platte High band can be heard playing in the gym. Although indoors and at least 200 feet away from the field, the Bulldog drums begin to slowly drown out JJ and his PA. The VPH drums are throbbing with such intensity, some in the stands mistake the pounding for the yet-to-arrive Southern University corps.

At 5:30 p.m., the much-anticipated game day atmosphere everyone talks about comes together like the pieces to the hoped-for Tetris puzzle. Sparky, the Dalmatian dog belonging to the local firehouse, begins to roam the sidelines and mingle with the crowd. Opposite his position on the field is a creature slightly more mythological.

It's the bear.

Well, maybe not *the* Ville Platte bear, but his more cartoonish, anthropomorphic cousin.

The unofficial mascot of TCB X wears a split jersey, not unlike the split tee shirt Dr. Tim wore earlier. This time, instead of dividing loyalties between Sacred Heart and Ville Platte, the bruin's jersey proclaims love for two favorite NFL teams.

On the back of the half-New Orleans Saints/ half Chicago Bears jersey, the name of the creature is revealed. He is 'Bobby A. Bear'.

While Bobby and Sparky make friends with the crowd, two signs go up in the stadium – one from Coca-Cola, one from Wal-Mart.

The Coca-Cola banner is one of their mass-marketed 'Coca-Cola: Football Town USA' announcements that are printed *en masse* and can be seen at almost every high school stadium in the country. Even though the sign's slogan was surely made up in some high-rise boardroom somewhere by an advertising agent who probably never even heard of Ville Platte, the phrase seems to be a totally appropriate and accurate declaration for tonight.

The Wal-Mart banner, hanging from a fire truck, is a bit more personal in origin. The tarp is scrawled with the announcement: "Wal-Mart welcomes Southern University, October 6th, 2009 Tee Cotton Bowl."

On the field is the huddled Cracked pyrotechnics team. D-Day will be soon.

Strolling the track is Jesse James West, Sr., cane in hand, there to see his son's final prep game.

Jacob Fontenot takes a deep breath and smiles. "Everything is running smooth right now," he says proudly. "We've got parking. We've got the bear roaming. We've got the pyrotechnics team here.

"Check out the atmosphere. It's great right now!"

It is impossible to disagree, at least when facing westward. At the moment, the Sacred Heart stands remain somewhat empty, while the VPH home stands are already almost at capacity.

Fortunately, the vacancy sign that hangs on the visitors' side of the stadium is only temporary. At six o'clock, Trojan Nation does a flash mob-worthy entrance as the Blue and Gold flood in. In a blink of an eye, the visitor's side transforms from a few curious early birds to standing room only. Behind the Sacred Heart bleachers is a police escort leading the SHS pep squad into the stadium. Instead of the big yellow limousines that normally ferry them to away games, the Trojan crew decides to walk the distance – about two-thirds of a mile from one school to the other.

Jennifer Vidrine, the Bulldogs' self-proclaimed biggest fan, makes her way to the press box thirty minutes later. A 70's era homecoming queen from Ville Platte High, she seems to have lost none of the qualities befitting of the title. Long black locks still flow over a melt-worthy smile. The tones she speaks come out in only two flavors: either unquestionable congeniality or unbridled enthusiasm.

It's good to see her here; she has the ability to raise the level of energy in a room – or a stadium – just by being present.

Observing her enthusiasm for the game, one cannot help but notice that Ms. Vidrine and Dr. Tim are the proverbial two sides to the same community coin. Both grew up in Ville Platte in the same era. Dr. Tim attended Sacred Heart; Ms. Vidrine, Ville Platte High. Both have an incredible love for their community and are deeply involved in improving the lives of their town's citizens. Any city, regardless of size, would be fortunate to have one such advocate roaming inside their incorporated limits. This small town not only has two such angels, but two angels that feed off of each other's positive spirits.

While Tim and Jennifer are quite complementary, they are not identical. This is never as clear as in their manner of dress for the evening.

Tonight, whereas Dr. Tim displays neutrality in his customized polo shirt that bears the TCB emblem, but neither school's colors, his press box counterpart makes no such self-imposed restriction. Ms. Vidrine dons VPH violet from head-to-toe. With a glamorous purple pantsuit and frilly white blouse, she looks as if she'd just stepped off stage with the rest of Prince and the Revolution, circa 1985.

Jennifer grabs the press box microphone to announce the arrival of tonight's special guests.

Her voice going full throttle, she yells, *"The 'S' on their chest means they are the best!"*

The switch is definitely set on 'unbridled enthusiasm'.

Southern University's drum line marches in on her cue, all high steps and pride as if they'd be performing at the Bayou Classic rather than down the bayou.

After the Jaguars quiet down, members and family representatives of the legendary 1965 Ville Platte High team make their way to the fifty-yard line. The sounds of 'Catch Me If You Can' and 'Gonna Fly Now (The Rocky Theme)' blare out of worn stadium speakers. A purple cart races to the center, carrying more representatives of the undefeated squad.

While game balls are being handed out to honorees, a single light glows above the stadium. Chatter in the crowd swells as people try to predict if it's a lucky star or just the plane carrying promised skydivers.

One by one, jumpers spill out of the plane. A hazy mist covers the field, making the landings even more dramatic. The illusion of divers materializing from out of nowhere provides more than one gasp from the audience.

The fourth (and last) parachutist has tethered an American flag to his black jumpsuit. His touchdown landing, a possibly unintentional slide into the end zone, gives the signal for the teams to approach the field.

Through the PA system, the crowd hears a foreign but familiar chant:

"Ka mate! Ka mate! Ka ora! Ka ora!"

It's Haka time.

The seniors from each squad menacingly stomp towards the middle of the field as they mimic the Maori war cry and rugby ritual.

The New Zealand version of the march is guaranteed to end in taunting and glowering of the teams at the bottom of the bowl. The Tee Cotton Bowl version, historically, tends to end in high-fives and celebration.

Tonight, however, the two teams put aside the normal post-Haka protocol. The stomp instead will terminate in a bow and a prayer by both teams, as the Tee Cotton Bowl pauses to reflect on the previous day's ambush in Fort Hood, Texas. Remembrance is given to the dozen soldiers who lost their lives when Major Nidal Malik Hasan opened fire at a military processing center there.

After the moment of silence comes the moment of 'BOOM!'

Almost 10 minutes' worth of fireworks launch into the night sky. The smell of gunpowder from the explosions pierces a clear, mild evening.

Perfect weather for gumbo. Perfect weather for football.

Perfect.

The only way the night could be more ideal for a football fan is if that fan were wearing purple. Once the game starts, the Bulldogs quickly gained a thirst to hold the Vidrine Cup high for the third consecutive year. By half time, they will have built a commanding 29-6 lead. In the first two quarters, senior Bulldog quarterback Cody Jones would methodically slice through the Trojan defense with a pair of six-point scampers and two touchdown tosses. A single Trojan score registers thanks to a quick carry by quarterback Stuart Schexnayder.

The tilted mid-point scoreboard tosses Jennifer Vidrine into overdrive. The Bulldog alum's joy is overwhelming as she announces the Southern drum line half time show. The press box microphone might as well serve as a prop as she loudly introduces the heartbeat of the 'Human Jukebox.'

"Superior! Superlative! Sensational!" she shouts.

"Southern University! Show them some love!"

Randy Guillory of KVPI describes the jamming Jaguars' performance to his listeners quite accurately when he proclaims, "If you saw the movie *Drumline*, these guys are putting them to shame."

On the field, the drum corps back up Vidrine's kindly accurate words. Between the high kicks and head flings, eight tom drummers flick sticks at each other while keeping time.

As if the night weren't surreal enough, during the Jags' halftime exit, Immi Jimmi M.J. sneaks onto the field for one last Reader's Digest version of 'Thriller'.

Afterwards, an SU band member is heard exclaiming, "I feel the love in the atmosphere here!"

With halftime festivities over, VPH put the hard hats back on. In repeat performances from the first half, the Bulldogs kept pounding while the good doctor would keep running.

At 9 p.m., well into the fourth quarter, Dr. Tim bounces to the press box to ask for a cart for an injured player. He also says farewell to the Saints-Tampa Bay tickets from his personal season ticket stash as a name is drawn from a hat.

On his way down, he carries the Vidrine Cup.

Shortly after 9:20 p.m., the scoreboard is forever sealed at 41-12. The Bulldogs take away the trophy for the third straight season. Team quarterbacks Jones and Schexnayder, who each added six-point donations on scrams in the second half, take home respective MVP honors.

Players from both squads linger on the field, chatting and congratulating each other. Dr. Tim's mantra of "talk good about your opponents; talk good about your teammates; let others talk good about you" is written all over the post-game formalities.

At 9:47 p.m., Dr. Tim packs up the circus he has brought with him once a year for the past 10 years. Up for almost 19 hours at this point, he still hasn't found the ability to stop and rest nor the desire to ask for help.

Like an incognito worker bee, Fontenot quietly, methodically loads his SUV with the relics and leftovers from the big day. Although he easily could summon help from the parents, players, and volunteers still mulling about, he is quite satisfied with only the assistance of his son, Jacob.

Sometime after 10 p.m., the Chevy – packed as tight as it was when it drove into the stadium at 7 a.m. – pulls out of the gated stadium area. Right behind the vehicle, slowly scooting like a Sandcrawler stuck in first gear, is Joe Cahn's RV of Tailgating Doom.

"When you can have a score that was like that, and the kids can still joke and be happy and you didn't see anything bad going on, it's a success," Dr. Tim reflects as he leaves.

Prior to the season, Dr. Tim described what drives him to put on such a big deal for such a small town.

"Every kid deserves to play in a big game," he said back in August, proudly talking about his brainstorms like a man on a mission.

For TCB X, mission accomplished.

CHAPTER TEN

A Peek Into the Future

A family tradition of the Fontenots is the table gathering that occurs in the wee hours after the Tee Cotton Bowl. Around the kitchen table, exhausted from the night's festivities but savoring the last drop of adrenaline from the week, Tim and Timbo begin their first of a year-long series of ping-pong sessions. As soon as they return from the game, the men ricochet one brainstorm after another off each other as they attempt to answer the driving perpetual question:

"What in heck can we do to top this?"

What has been berthed from these conversations in the past decade has been quite incredible. It may just be easier to list things in old-school *New Testament* style.

For example, when talking about TCB activities, to paraphrase the Gospel of Matthew, we can say that the purchase of a trophy begat fireworks, which begat NFL Films, which begat the pre-game banquet, which begat live concerts, which begat the Haka, which begat appearances by Southern University's drumline, which begat Joe Cahn's cross-country boudin runs, which begat skydivers, which begat....

Washerboards?

Yes, washerboards. A simple game played by physical education students where hardware washers are tossed into holes in wooden boxes.

In fact, the idea for a future Tee Cotton Week washerboard tourney came to Dr. Tim and Jacob even before they made it home from TCB X.

"By accident, a washerboard game got left out on the field from a P.E. class, and little kids would run out and play during the (Tee Cotton Bowl)," Tim describes as he introduces a mental note made from the press box. "I said that was great, that's awesome. I said next year we're going to have a washerboard competition. We're going to take students from each school that are not on the (football) teams. We're going to take the two winners from each school and have them compete at halftime. We'll have washerboards on each side of the field for the little kids to play. They'll play with Bobby A. Bear, Sparky the Dog. We might even give a Tee Cotton Bowl washerboard as one of the prizes."

A Tee Cotton-themed washerboard would be a prize to be cherished if the effort going into decorating the game box were equal to the amount of work that goes into decorating the loads of official Tee Cotton Bowl game balls handed out over the years. The prized pigskins – decorated by Tim, Jacob, and student volunteers and handed out as awards to dignitaries and Hall of Fame members – have become highly treasured items and somewhat of a folk art cottage industry of its own.

But after NFL Film features and Papal blessings, shouldn't the good doctor be trying to pluck a few more stars from the sky? Shouldn't Tee Cotton be trying for more 'Wow!' and less 'Washerboard'?

Not really.

"It doesn't have to be bigger; it just has to be better," the founder says shyly. "If it's bigger, it might not be us."

With a little coaxing, however, Dr. Tim starts revealing a less-modest Christmas list. The Cajun tongue becomes a little looser as Fontenot picks bigger goodies from the corner of his mind.

"Camo jerseys!" he eventually shouts out like a game show contestant blurting a last-second winning answer. "That's something that hasn't come to realization. I would love to have camo jerseys. That clock is ticking really fast (for this year). If it doesn't occur, that's okay, but I'd love for the kids to have white jerseys with camo numbers for the visiting team and the home team to have camo jerseys with white numbers, because of Squirrel Day and stuff."

At that point, Tim reaches further into his crystal ball for some more fantasy picks.

"I'd still like to get a jet flyover, or to get a Blackhawk helicopter to come down... maybe a Ranger to slide down with the game ball. I'll wait (to ask) until the economy gets better and the government has more money to spend. They can join up with us and get some good publicity."

He even dares mention the 'M' word.

"A movie is still big on my list... Denzel, if you're out there, we've got a story to be told!"

Ten years later, Dr. Tim still likes dropping names and dropping lines. His current list of potential pen pals includes Nike, Adidas, Bob Ryan of the *Boston Globe*, and even a few addresses in New Zealand. While he's heard nothing significant back from those recipients yet, he's not pouting when the postman arrives empty-handed.

"I send out so many lines... if it doesn't come back, then it wasn't meant to be."

One of his more recent letters that received a bite was from the nation of South Africa. *Invictus* is a story that the good doctor considers a muse.

"I wrote (Nelson) Mandela. His people wrote me back and said they like what we stand for. What he did for a nation, we did with a town."

Jacob mentions that *Invictus* is not the only flick to find itself in Tee Cotton roots.

"It's like we get a lot of inspirations from movies, quotes, and all that. One of the great quotes we always say from the Matrix is, 'No one's ever tried this before. That's why it's going to work.'"

And work it has. Work so well, that doubting the future potential for this game is an exercise in futility.

"My friends just call themselves the Apostles," jokes Jacob, explaining how his friends have given up trying to limit the TCB. "They just believe."

Dr. Tim hopes the Tee Cotton concept will spread to other towns both inside and outside of the state of Louisiana. If the adage *'Imitation is the sincerest form of flattery'* holds true, he hopes that in years to come, business people and visionaries from all over will afford him this type of praise.

"They wouldn't be stealing from me," he says as he wishes that other entrepreneurs would get the *ahnvee* [32] to set up such a shop in their own backyards. "I steal from other people, too," Fontenot confesses, explaining where some of his ideas come from. He cites the friendly rivalry between West Jones and Wayne County high schools in the neighboring state of Mississippi as inspiration. "They respect each other; I like them. We're a lot like them.

"That's why God has us to do this, so others will pick up on it. I'd like other schools to do it. I won't feel jealous."

Finally, after a decade of planting seeds on the football field, both Tim and Timbo are anxious to see the results of some very faithful farming.

"It's becoming more ingrained in the kids and the future of the community," Jacob assesses. "The kids play the game this way because it's the only way they know how to play the game – with the respect that they show for each other. They play that way because that's the way it's supposed to be."

His dad adds, "What I'm happy about is that we are more than just talk. We are more than a game; we walk the walk. We do what we are supposed to do, and the game proves it. I tell the kids all the time, 'I will always point back to

---

[32] **Ahnvee** (*ON-vee*) a Cajun term meaning to have a temptation or urge

you, that this is how the game is supposed to be. You set the bar high.'

"This is how you see competition, that you don't hate somebody, you love them. And because you love them, you give them your best. You don't pound yourself on the chest. When you're humble, you don't have to beat yourself on the chest. You know you're good."

After that comment Tim says, "I'm anxious to see when kids who played this game have kids of their own, how they will address this game."

Even now, the Tee Cotton spirit has spread. In other sports, including softball and other girls' sports, the teams will gather for prayer and pizza after the games. There's been *Tee Tee Cotton* and *Tee Cotton Jr.* games for the junior varsity and junior high football teams. A prize one year for the younger grades was not a mounted two-handled chalice, but a thimble filled with cotton.

"About all the cotton they can handle," Tim laughs.

Satisfied with their peek into the future, father and son take a quick glance into the past and all that has been accomplished.

"I've come to expect the unexpected," Jacob realizes. "Don't ever set a limit on what the game might become."

For Dr. Tim, the credit all goes to the Tee Cotton's Biggest Fan.

"I think I broke my loaves and my fish and had no idea what He could do when He took it in and multiplied it," Fontenot points out. "I had no idea, but God had a plan. He took my ideas. He said you give Me the credit and I'll give you the results. You stop giving Me the credit, and I'll stop giving you the results.

"We just thought it was just a little fun game; we had no idea. We have to think outside the box. We can't put God inside the box."

He adds, "One man told me, 'Some people may never go to church, but they can go to a football game and see God there. You might be the only Bible they ever read. You're taking God out the church and putting him in the streets. It's a joy.'"

There's good reason for Dr. Tim to bring the G-man to a small-town football game. Seems the founder owes Him a few favors.

In 1987, when Tim first went to open up his own physical therapy practice, the contractor Fontenot hired to build his office ran off with $20,000 he'd paid to do the work.

In 1993, as business began to pour in and Dr. Tim had started work on a new home, an entirely unexpected contract issue with a local hospital threatened to cut off about 60% of his business.

In both cases, the Fontenot family dropped to their knees in prayer. The energy a person normally caught in these situations would eat up in anger, Tim and Suzy used to strengthen their faith.

Today, Fontenot is being interviewed in one of two offices he owns. For this chapter of *Sharpened Iron*, the sports nut answers questions in an examination room overflowing with memorabilia, evidence of sports treks from New Orleans to New Zealand.

The Maxwell Football Club member is living the gridiron lover's dream. He still has the privilege of roaming the sidelines as a trainer for his college alma mater, McNeese State, and has his own stash of Saints season tickets. He routinely stays in touch with Steve Sabol and David Swain of NFL Films, the *Commish*, and a handful of journalists from around the U.S.

While he is living a football fanatics' fantasy, Fontenot is not flying solo; he is bringing a city along with him. He has provided his town – a town whose entire population *might* fill the bottom bowl of a professional basketball arena – with a football game whose pageantry eclipses all but a few prime-time collegiate bowls and even some professional games.

Many times, he provides the high school athletes of the town with free services so they can afford to live their own dreams under stadium lights.

For this, he expects no credit for himself. Tim sees the God that put the eyes of NFL Films and Tony Dungy and Pope John Paul II on the TCB as the same God that helped him dig out of his own darkest hours in 1987 and 1993.

At our meeting, Tim Fontenot is surrounded by framed autographs, dozens of miniature football helmets, and even an autographed rugby ball. We talk for hours inside an office that never should have been built for a business that never should have succeeded, discussing a game that for all sakes and purposes should not be taking place.

In the middle of conversation, Dr. Tim leans in and looks directly at this author with one simple reminder.

"God can do everything but fail. Give God the glory, and He'll give you the results.

"Quote me exactly."

EPILOGUE

Long after the interviews were over and I was in the middle of editing, an incredible event struck the Ville Platte community. Although what occurred was devistating, the unity of the townspeople prevented it from becoming more of a tragedy.

Not mentioned in any chapter of *Sharpened Iron* was the difficult challenge God had set before the family of Ville Platte High coach Roy Serie. At the time this book was being written, Coach Serie's wife, Shelia, was in the last stages of her battle with breast cancer.

It was her determined wish to live long enough to see her daughter, Kiera, graduate high school.

On May 5, 2010, just eight days before her daughter was to walk across the stage, Sheila died in a car accident coming home from M.D. Anderson Hospital in Houston.

Coach Serie was driving. The head-on collision also took the life of the other driver. Roy and a passenger from the other vehicle were both briefly hospitalized.

A few days after his wife's death, the coach sent Dr. Tim a text message that read: "Did you see what the Tee Cotton Bowl is doing?"

When I had asked him what exactly he meant, Serie said, "To put it frankly, I couldn't believe how many white faces were coming through the door (of the hospital) – doctors, lawyers, kids in Sacred Heart jerseys. The whole community was showing unity.

"Honestly, when this thing (the Tee Cotton Bowl) first started, it was a competition. The vision Dr. Tim had, nobody saw. This thing is bigger than anybody could see. The people that weren't into the message and the love – at the funeral, they saw that this is not a joke."

The outpouring of love from the Sacred Heart community kept coming for the 'rival' school's coach, too.

On the afternoon of Kiera's graduation, Mitzi McDaniel, mother of Sacred Heart's Cade McDaniel, waited by Coach Serie's doorstep for him to come home. She had several items with her, including a picture of Cade, a letter from a lady that benefitted from Cade's organ donations, and a piece of jewelry as a gift for Kiera. The 'Heart-to-Heart' had two rubies: one to represent Cade and another to represent Sheila.

By the coach's recollection, Ms. McDaniel had also brought a dinner of "the best roast beef I'd ever eaten."

Serie reminded me that "had it not been for the Tee Cotton Bowl, she (Mrs. McDaniel) would never have walked through the door."

To reciprocate the generosity, Coach Serie wrote a poem for Cade. The Ville Platte High coach was known to give his own senior track athletes a sendoff in stanzas; this was the first time he would honor a Sacred Heart athlete with the same. The poem, which he would read at the SHS graduation, started off by honoring Cade but ended up honoring Mitzi McDaniel and the entire Trojan community.

In part, it read:

> *That's your mother, Mrs. McDaniel*
> *Who inspired me to do this*
> *You're one of the strongest women I've ever met*
> *What you did for my daughter*
> *I'll never forget*

You sat in the sun on the porch with your phone
While Cade and Shelia are smiling in their new home
I love you Mrs. McDaniel
And the Sacred Heart Community
Who would ever say that
We could come together in unity
What we must remember through all that we learn
The things we want most are the things we gotta earn

APPENDIX

(Photo Credit:Bobby Dardeau)

Two teams, literally, from across the tracks. Seated and smiling between the Sacred Heart (left) and Ville Platte High (right) members is Tee Cotton Bowl founder Tim Fontenot.

(Photo Credit Bobby Dardeau)
Even cheerleaders are friendly foes in the TCB 'war'.

(Photo Credit: Bruce Campbell)
The famed Southern University drum line at TCB X.

(Photo Credit: Bobby Dardeau)

Both teams gather together in prayer for the pre-game banquet. Athletes are told to pray for their opponents to play at their best.

(Photo Credit: Bruce Campbell)

After the game, both teams hug it out.

(Photo Credit: Mike Fuselier)

Celebrity Tailgating Commissioner Joe Cahn inspects a bowl of Cajun goodness during Tee Cotton IX. Cahn, who for the past fifteen years has attended the parking lot parties of over 500 sporting events, is a repeat visitor to Ville Platte and the Tee Cotton Bowl.

(Photo Credit: Bruce Campbell)
Sacred Heart quarterback Stuart Schexnayder and Ville Platte High quarterback Cody Jones pose for the TCB X Media Guide.

(Photo Credit: Mike Fuselier)
A skydiver, toting the American flag, comes in for a landing during TCB IX.

(Photo Credit: Bruce Campbell)
Unofficial Tee Cotton good-luck charm Tracy 'Big-T' Jagneaux listens to a speech by Dr. Tim while giving a hug to his daughter, Kelsy. Standing behind them is Tim's son and Tee Cotton co-founder, Jacob Fontenot.

(Photo Credit: Mike Fuselier/ de la Claire Fine Arts)

Fireworks go off behind the goalposts during Tee Cotton Bowl VI. As the game grows, so does the pageantry. Fans nowadays can expect nothing less than a full ten minutes of the sparkly stuff right before kickoff.

(Photo Credit: Bruce Campbell)

The Jesse James gang walks proudly during TCB X. Here, Jesse James West Jr. (right), a Ville Platte High player in the contest, carries a game ball decorated for his father, West Sr. (left), who was inducted into the Tee Cotton Bowl Hall Of Fame in a pre-game ceremony that night.

(Photo Credit: Bruce Campbell)

In keeping with TCB tradition, The Ville Platte High seniors challenge Sacred Heart with the Haka in the TCB X pregame. The Haka, originally a Maori war cry from the aboriginal tribes of New Zealand, is a popular taunt performed between rival rugby teams.

(Photo Credit: Bruce Campbell)

Both teams gather around Dr. Tim Fontenot after Tee Cotton X. Here, the good doctor makes it a point to thank the teams for their sportsmanship and to remind them what the game and their efforts mean to the Ville Platte community.

(Photo Credit: Bruce Campbell)

Both teams pile around the Jerome Vidrine Cup after Tee Cotton X. In the middle of the chaos, embracing the hardware, is VPH's Cole LeCoq. At the top of the picture, an athlete from each squad helps lift up Cade McDaniel's #20 jersey.

(Photo Credit: Bruce Campbell)

(Photo Credit: Mike Fuselier)

The spirit of helping 'the other guy' is reflected both in the design of the MVP trophy and the on-field action.

(Photo courtesy of the Fontenot family collection)

Former NFL coach and best-selling author Tony Dungy accepts the gift of a hand-painted Tee Cotton Bowl game ball from the crew on their visit to Indianapolis in 2009. Pictured are (L to R): Tee Cotton co-founder Jacob Fontenot, Ville Platte High head coach Roy Serie, Tony Dungy, Sacred Heart head coach Dutton Wall, and Tee Cotton founder 'Dr. Tim' Fontenot.

A TCB TIMELINE

2000
Tee Cotton I
Site: Soileau-Landry Field

Sacred Heart 24
Ville Platte High 21

- First fireworks
- First awarding of the traveling Vidrine Cup

2001
Tee Cotton II
Site: Ville Platte High Stadium

Sacred Heart 33
Ville Platte High 6

- "Tee Cotton II Brings Community Together" column appears in Daily World

---

2002
Tee Cotton III
Site: Soileau-Landry Field

Sacred Heart 26
Ville Platte High 12

- Tee Cotton Hall of Fame established
- First Tee Cotton Banquet (Louisiana State University/ Cincinnati Bengal standout Tommy Casanova guest speaker)
- Tee Cotton Bowl story developed into a feature for ESPN by NFL Films

2003
Tee Cotton IV
Site: Ville Platte High Stadium

Sacred Heart 42
Ville Platte High 6

- McNeese State University drum line performs at halftime
- First Tee Cotton Bowl Jr. event for junior varsity teams
- Tee Cotton Bowl wins the *Louisiana Community Quarterback* award sponsored by Parade Magazine and The United Way

---

2004
Tee Cotton V
Site: Soileau-Landry Field

Sacred Heart 38
Ville Platte High 18

- Banquet guest speaker: pro wrestler Ernie 'Big Cat' Ladd
- McNeese State University and Louisiana Blues Brothers band appear for halftime
- Tee Cotton game receives official Papal blessings from Pope John Paul II

2005
Tee Cotton VI
Site: Ville Platte High Stadium

Sacred Heart 31
Ville Platte High 30

- Special note: halftime score was 0-0; game wound up being decided in triple-overtime.
- Banquet guest speaker: Los Angeles Dodger Danny Ardoin

- Also for banquet was a special recorded message for both teams by Steve Sabol, president of NFL Films
- Food drive held at game for victims of Hurricanes Katrina and Rita

---

2006
Tee Cotton VII
Site: Soileau-Landry Field

Sacred Heart 27
Ville Platte High 6

- First Haka (performed by Ville Platte High)
- First Tee Cotton Bowl to be broadcast via World Wide Web

2007
Tee Cotton VIII
Site: Ville Platte High Stadium

Ville Platte High 48
Sacred Heart 14

- Special note: Former Ville Platte High athlete Tracy 'Big T' Jagneaux, an assistant coach at Sacred Heart for first seven Tee Cotton Bowls, takes a job at Ville Platte High as an assistant, thus beginning his reputation as the Tee Cotton's good-luck charm.
- First Haka (performed by both teams)
- First community prayer service for game
- First TCB prayer breakfast

2008
Tee Cotton IX
Site: Soileau-Landry Field

Ville Platte High 34
Sacred Heart 27

- First appearance of 'Tailgating Commisioner' Joe Cahn at the Tee Cotton Bowl
- First appearance of skydivers
- Tee-Tee Cotton Bowl played between Jr. High teams for the TCB thimble

---

2009
Tee Cotton X
Site: Ville Platte High Stadium

Ville Platte High 41
Sacred Heart 12

- Banquet guest speaker: Super Bowl referee Greg Gautreaux
- Tee Cotton Bowl honored by Tyndale House and Tony Dungy in the *Win A Day Of Uncommon Service* contest.
- First appearance of 'Bobby A. Bear'
- Ville Platte High undefeated team of 1965 honored
- Halftime performance by Southern University drum line

A LOTTA STUFFIS FROM THE AUTHOR
(no, that's not a typo – just the obligatory obscure reference)

Special thanks:

- A big shout out to Woody Gunnels, Philip Gachassin, J.J. Vincent and Michelle George for helping me hold it all together when I needed you guys.
- Much love to Paul Radke, Darrel Kirsch, and Steve Silvo for past guidance that still sticks around today.
- Endless thanks to Maria and Mike Hebert for the use of the hideout so I could write this sucker in peace.
- High-fives to the Hampton Inns in Jennings and Natchitoches (go NSU!) when the Hebert hideout wasn't available.
- Tip of the hat to Dr. Tim Fontenot for all the 'pop quizzes' you've had to answer over the past year. How in the world do you remember all of this stuff?
- Appreciation to anyone in the Ville Platte community who let me swipe a photo or steal a story to add to this book.
- Lastly, the biggest hug in the world to AngelButt, CrackHead, and Snuffy. (I really have to find better nicknames for my family).

Websites:
For more stuff by the author:
www.goMELgo.com
www.facebook.com/goMELgo
For Maxwell Football Club updates:
www.maxwellfootballclub.org
Information about the *Baskets of Hope* charity:
www.basketsofhope.org
To follow Joe Cahn:
www.tailgating.com

To keep up with the town of Ville Platte
-Ville Platte Gazette
www.villeplattetoday.com
-Bonne Nouvelles magazine
www.ilovegoodnews.com
-KVPI
www.Oldies925.com

About the front and back covers:

Awesome front cover concept/photography courtesy of Bobby Dardeau. Thanks for making me (well, my book) look so good!

On the back cover, the Ville Platte High players meet up with Sacred Heart players on the Trojans' practice field to pray after hearing of Cade McDaniel's passing. The Bulldogs actually suspended their own practice immediately upon hearing the news so they could join SHS in mourning. (From the McDaniel family collection, photo by Tammy Parrott).

Egotistical stuff the author wanted you to know:

      Mel LeCompte, Jr. has previously appeared in numerous publications in South Louisiana including: Opelousas *Daily World*, Lafayette *Daily Advertiser*, Ville Platte *Gazette*, *SportsWrap* magazine and *Purple and Gold* magazine. In his two years of awards eligibility while working part-time at the Daily World, he picked up two awards for his sports columns, including the LA-MS Associated Press award (first place, 2001). He also took home three awards for cartoons, including the Louisiana Press Association Best Editorial Cartoon award (first place in 2000 and 2001, competing against all dailies).
      He still loves the cartoon thing, and has written and illustrated a children's book, *The Ice Cream Cow*. After a brief respite, Mel plans to complete a Louisiana-centric kiddie tome that celebrates life in all corners of the Pelican state, from the Big Easy to Big Mamou.

Made in the USA
Columbia, SC
12 August 2022

65238512R00133